10 Performance-Based
STEM Projects

Grades 6–8

10

Performance-Based
STEM Projects

Todd Stanley

PRUFROCK PRESS INC.
WACO, TEXAS

Prufrock Press Inc.
P.O. Box 8813
Waco, TX 76714-8813
Phone: (800) 998-2208
Fax: (800) 240-0333
http://www.prufrock.com

INTRODUCTION

Why Project-Based Learning?

When my assistant principal, Dr. Jones, would visit my science and social studies class and observe the project-based learning (PBL) my students were engaged in, he would always ask in the post-conference, "How do you know it is working?" To me, this seemed like asking someone why water is wet. It just is. Through the day-to-day observations, I could see that my students were more engaged and learning more through project-based learning than the traditional teaching methods I had used during the first 5 years of my teaching career. Were their test results better at the end of the year? Yes, but more important than this quantitative data was the qualitative data my students provided me. My students would come to visit me after having left for the high school and say, "High school is easy because we used project learning in your class. I knew how to research, I knew how to present, and I remembered the material we learned." When students and their parents would talk about their later schooling experiences, they were always grateful we had done project-based learning because it better prepared them for the future.

Despite these stories, Dr. Jones would always resist: "Where's the research to back up that this is working in the classroom?" This was right at the beginning of the data explosion in education, and I did not have any research to tell me it was working. I just *knew* it was working. Again, Dr. Jones would challenge me: "If you had research to back this up, it would make the power of its effectiveness much better because it would be quantifiable."

Since these conversations, project-based learning has been slowly but surely making its way into the educational conversation. Documentaries such as *Most Likely to Succeed* (Dintersmith & Whiteley, 2015) show the power PBL can have on students. As PBL has gained traction in schools, there has been more and more research on its effectiveness. Not only did I know it was working, but I could also back it up with study after study.

How Effective Is Problem-Based Learning?

When Thomas (2000) reviewed research on PBL, he found evidence that using it in the classroom enhanced the quality of student learning, especially when compared to other methods of instruction. Specifically, he saw that PBL was effective for teaching processes, such as problem solving and decision making. Boaler (2002) looked at two British secondary schools that had a similar student makeup. One of these schools used traditional methods to teach mathematics. The other focused on project-based learning. Across 3 years of data, students in the project-based learning school outperformed the traditional school's students in mathematics, with 3 times as many students scoring the highest possible grade on the national examination (Boaler, p. 16). More than that, PBL better taught conceptual and applied knowledge, meaning there was a much better chance of enduring understanding.

In a more recent study, Deitering (2016) looked at whether project-based learning was a more effective instructional method than traditional teaching methods. She compared two groups, one taught through PBL and one taught through more traditional methods. Figure 1 summarizes her findings. Each group completed a science unit on rocks and erosion, followed by a reflection, which required students to consider three levels of engagement—retreatism, compliance, and engagement. The results of the student surveys showed that traditional instruction resulted in better student compliance. When students sit in perfectly positioned rows and are talked *at* for great lengths, it only makes sense that they would be compliant. Traditional methods were also higher in retreatism, but this is not a good thing. Retreatism is when students are disengaged from current classroom activities and goals. Although they are compliant, they are thinking about other things, causing them to reject both the official goals

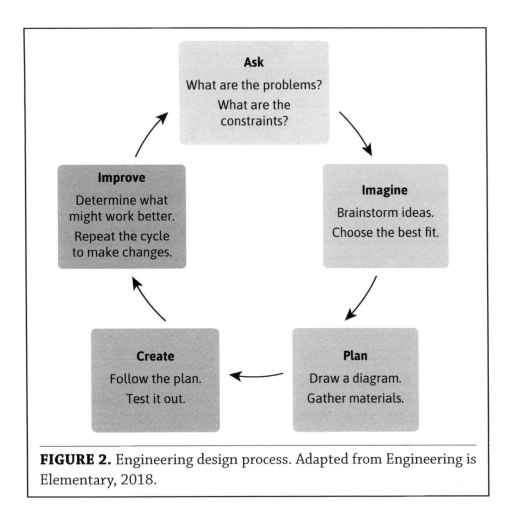

FIGURE 2. Engineering design process. Adapted from Engineering is Elementary, 2018.

The engineering design process gives students a good, solid model to follow, which can be applied throughout STEM areas as well as to social studies, art, and even gym class. Once students are familiar with the engineering design process, they will intrinsically revert to it whenever they are working on something. This is the true value of STEM learning.

Why STEM and PBL?

STEM-based PBL naturally lends itself to the formation of 21st-century skills, which are crucial to students' development in school and beyond. STEM learning engages students and equips them with critical thinking, problem solving, creative, and collaborative skills. Because of the authentic nature of STEM-based PBL experiences and the final products that students create, students also develop communication skills as well as self-direction. STEM and PBL create a perfect marriage in ensuring students are ready to be the leaders of tomorrow.

How This Book Is Organized

This book features 10 projects. Each project is linked to national STEM education goals. In selecting projects and the skills that they emphasize, I utilized the STEM Learning Goals and the System Dynamics and Systems Thinking Tools and Learning Strategies that make up effective STEM education, according to Creative Learning Exchange (2016; see Figure 3), as a framework. Projects are also based on and aligned to the Next Generation Science Standards and the Common Core State Standards for the target grade levels. Alignment charts are provided at the end of the book.

Each project focuses on a selected skill crucial to STEM learning; however, note that additional goals, big ideas, and essential questions are outlined in the introduction to each project:

- ▸ **Project 1:** Communicate effectively.
- ▸ **Project 2:** Focus on inquiry and collaboration.
- ▸ **Project 3:** Understand multiple content areas.
- ▸ **Project 4:** Explore contemporary issues.
- ▸ **Project 5:** Use technology, math, and reasoning.
- ▸ **Project 6:** Use and analyze models.
- ▸ **Project 7:** Record and analyze data.
- ▸ **Project 8:** Investigate change over time and patterns.
- ▸ **Project 9:** Use computer models or simulations.
- ▸ **Project 10:** Construct and explain systems.

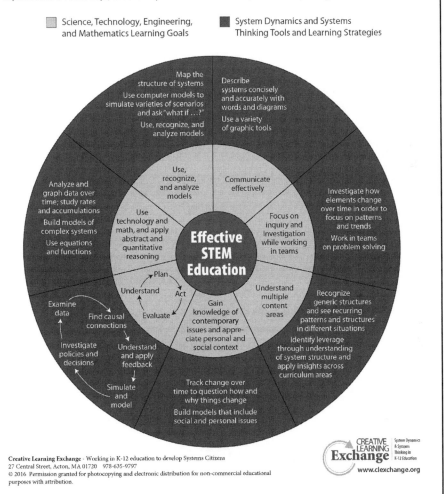

FIGURE 3. Effective STEM education. From "Using System Dynamics and Systems Thinking (SD/ST) Tools and Learning Strategies to Build Science, Technology, Engineering, and Math Excellence," by Creative Learning Exchange, 2016, retrieved from http://www.clexchange.org/curriculum/standards/stem.asp. Copyright 2016 by Creative Learning Exchange. Reprinted with permission.

1 Communicate Effectively

The ability to communicate effectively—both verbally and in writing—is crucial to our students during their time in our classrooms and beyond. Consider a lawyer. He has to be able to write legal briefs that enable him to build his case. He also needs to communicate these briefs to the judge or court in order to effectively represent his client. Doctors also use a combination of these skills. They have to be able to communicate effectively with their patients in order to explain what is going on, and they have to record what they learned into patients' files so that there is an established record of patients' health. These are simplified examples, but that does not diminish the importance of communication skills.

Teachers, especially, utilize communication in their profession, from teaching concepts to a class, to communicating with parents, administrators, and other stakeholders, and more. If a teacher is effectively going to provide feedback to students, he or she must be able to convey this feedback both in written and verbal form. This double reinforcement better equips students to learn from mistakes and strive for improvement in the future.

What does communication look like in a STEM project? It can take a variety of forms, depending on the product that students are asked to produce. For example, if students have been charged with defending a proposal for a design for a product they wish to market to an authentic panel, they will have to employ their speaking skills in order to effectively communicate their plan. Such a presentation requires a combination of style and substance—style in the manner in which the proposal is presented and substance in the quality of the information presented. Characteristics of high-quality presentations of this nature might include:

- The presentation can be clearly heard the entire time, and the participant speaks slowly and clearly throughout.
- The presenter's demeanor is professional throughout. It sounds as though the presentation has been rehearsed several times.
- The presentation is organized in a manner that makes it easy to follow and to understand what is going on at any given time.

If, however, students were charged with creating a brochure that conveyed the information for the project, they would have to communicate in written form. Characteristics of high-quality products of this nature might include:

- The brochure has little to no spelling/grammatical errors.
- The brochure is typed in a format that makes it easy to view.
- The brochure uses sentence structures that makes the paragraphs flow and easy to read.

No matter which style students are asked to communicate in, the substance needs to have the same quality. These descriptors could be used for either written or spoken products:

- The project is organized clearly, allowing someone to know what is being discussed at any given time.
- The student provides plenty of examples to back up statements made.
- The student provides much detail, explaining concepts and ideas so that someone can gain a full understanding of what is being talked about.

It is important that any project you present to students requires them to utilize both written and spoken skills so that students display competence in any venue. This will make them that much more effective when going out in the real world to find themselves a job. After all, the top job skills that companies are looking for in new hires all have to do with communication (Graduate Management Admission Council, 2018; see Figure 4). If you were to help your students master both written and verbal com-

1.	Oral communication	6.	Value opinions of others
2.	Listening skills	7.	Integrity
3.	Adaptability	8.	Follow a leader
4.	Written communication	9.	Drive
5.	Presentation skills	10.	Cross-cultural sensitivity

FIGURE 4. Top 10 skills sought by employers. Adapted from Graduate Management Admission Council, 2018.

munication, they would have an advantage over other potential hires who are less accomplished with these skills.

Logo Art Installation

In this project, students will work in groups to create an art installation and design a recognizable logo to represent their teacher's teaching team. A good installation will:

- ▸ pair well with the name of the program (if the program already has a name; alternatively, students could develop a name);
- ▸ express the program's personality;
- ▸ convey the type of business (an educational program) and what the program promotes;
- ▸ send a clear message;
- ▸ be accompanied by a strong tagline;
- ▸ have a logo that successfully works in black and white (for successful transfer to paper);
- ▸ feature a simple, clean design; and
- ▸ be memorable.

Students will present their final products to be judged by a panel of adults with firsthand knowledge of the teaching team (i.e., their teachers). Students may only use environmentally friendly or recycled materials to construct their installations. They may not purchase any materials, and a materials list must be on display when their installations are judged. Students' installations must fit within a space that is 3 feet by 4 feet by 6 inches (this is the maximum size—installations can be smaller).

Groups must also develop a presentation for the judges. Presentations need to be 3–5 minutes long, and all group members must speak. Presentations should include the group's design and model, a rationale for how the logo art installation represents the teaching team, and a display that indicates which materials were use in the creation of the installation.

Materials

- ▸ Student computer and Internet access
- ▸ Project Outline: Logo Art Installation (student copies)
- ▸ Suggested Timeline
- ▸ Lesson: What Makes a Logo Successful?
- ▸ Lesson: Recycled Artwork
- ▸ Handout 1.1: Logo Art Installation Design (student copies)
- ▸ Product Rubric: Logo Art Installation (student copies)

PROJECT OUTLINE

Logo Art Installation

Big Idea

A well-thought-out design can effectively communicate information.

Essential Question

How can a logo effectively represent an organization?

Deliverables

You will work with a group to create an art installation of a recognizable logo to represent your teacher's teaching team. A good installation will:

- pair well with the name of the program;
- express the program's personality;
- convey the type of business (an educational program) and what the program promotes;
- send a clear message;
- be accompanied by a strong tagline;
- have a logo that successfully works in black and white (for successful transfer to paper);
- feature a simple, clean design; and
- be memorable.

You will present your final product to be judged by a panel of adults with first-hand knowledge of the teaching team. You must develop a presentation for the judges. Presentations need to be 3–5 minutes long, and all group members must speak. Presentations should include your group's design and model, a rationale for how the logo art installation represents the teaching team, and a display that indicates which materials were use in the creation of the installation.

Members of your group will take on the following roles:

- **Project Manager:** Responsible for keeping the group on task, making sure deadlines are met, and making sure that all members are doing their parts.
- **Resource Manager:** Responsible for keep track of the materials needed to create the installation and displaying the materials list for the presentation.

Project Outline: Logo Art Installation, *continued*

▸ **Quality Control:** Responsible for ensuring project requirements are followed and determining if improvements need to be made.

Constraints

You must:
- ▸ only use environmentally friendly or recycled materials to construct your installation,
- ▸ not purchase any materials, and
- ▸ construct an installation that fits within a space that is 3 feet by 4 feet by 6 inches (this is the maximum size—installations can be smaller).

SUGGESTED TIMELINE

DAY				
1 Introduce the project and conduct Lesson: What Makes a Logo Successful? *Ask.*	**2** Divide students into groups to brainstorm logo ideas. *Imagine.*	**3** Have groups continue to brainstorm logo ideas. *Imagine.*	**4** Conduct Lesson: Recycled Artwork. *Ask.*	**5** Have groups draft their logo design. *Plan.*
6 Have groups discuss improvements that can be made to their designs. *Improve.*	**7** Have groups draw a final draft of their logo design. *Plan.*	**8** Have groups make a list of materials needed to create their logo and who will supply what. *Plan.*	**9** Have groups create their logos. *Create.*	**10** Have groups create their logos. *Create.*
11 Have groups create their logos. *Create.*	**12** Have groups create their logos. *Create.*	**13** Have groups work on their presentations. *Create.*	**14** Have groups practice their presentations. *Improve.*	**15** Have groups present their installations to judges.

Project 1: Communicate Effectively

LESSON

What Makes a Logo Successful?

1. Share with students some examples of iconic logos and see if they can name them (e.g., Starbucks, Nike, McDonald's, Amazon, Facebook, Apple, Target, YouTube, Twitter, etc.). Ask: *What makes these logos stand out?* Students may come up with answers such as:
   ▸ The logo/symbol is the name of the company (Apple, Target).
   ▸ An initial from the company's name makes up the logo (McDonald's, Facebook).
   ▸ The logo depicts something to do with the function of the company (YouTube, Twitter).
   ▸ The logo/symbol has become synonymous with the company (Nike, Starbucks).

2. Share with students some original logos of companies that have very different logos today, such as Amazon (https://www.fineprintart.com/art/history-of-the-amazon-logo), Shell (https://www.logodesignlove.com/shell-logo-design-evolution), and/or AT&T (http://logos.wikia.com/wiki/AT%26T). Ask: *How do you think these logos improved?* Students may come up with answers such as:
   ▸ Amazon's first logo doesn't really tell a viewer much about what the company does. The newer logo has the arrow showing that Amazon carries everything from A to Z.
   ▸ The first logo for Shell depicts a shell, but it is not very eye-catching. The second one is bright and visible.
   ▸ The older AT&T logos were probably very appropriate when phones were first in use and bells were actually used. The new logo shows a globe and the company's global reach.

3. Explain that as students create their logos, they need to consider:
   ▸ what the logo is going to look like,
   ▸ how the logo will attract people,
   ▸ how well it represents what the team stands for,
   ▸ if the logo can be easily used on letterheads and e-mails, and
   ▸ if people will identify with the logo.

Project 1: Communicate Effectively

LESSON

Recycled Artwork

1. Remind students that as they create their art installations, they will need to figure out what materials they want to work with.

2. Share with students how recycled materials can be used as art. You can display the slideshow available at https://www.slideshare.net/escuadraypincel/recycled-art-powerpoint. Alternatively, there are also some good YouTube videos, such as:

    ▸ "Artist Gives Recycled Materials New Life" (available at https://www.youtube.com/watch?v=ap9NFCiz4HI),

    ▸ "Is It Trash or Is It Art? Recycled Arts Festival" (available at https://www.youtube.com/watch?v=NkkjOhAhnLM), and

    ▸ "1,000 Recycled Bottle Art – Eden" (available at https://www.youtube.com/watch?v=69ulYseL0cw).

3. Tell students that their groups will need to decide how they are going to make the installation art and what materials they are going to need. Group members are responsible for bringing in the various materials.

Project 1: Communicate Effectively

HANDOUT 1.1

Logo Art Installation Design

Directions: To create your installation, you and your group will need to begin by drawing a design of what your installation will look like and what it will be made of.

Tips for Logo Art Installation Design

- ▶ Use graph paper or create the design on a computer.
- ▶ Use proper drawing tools (e.g., ruler, compass).
- ▶ Use a pencil for the initial drawing and then go over it with pen.
- ▶ Show more than one angle if possible.
- ▶ Include dimensions (i.e., how many inches and feet tall or wide the installation will be).
- ▶ Make sure the design is colorful and eye-catching.
- ▶ Make sure the design represents what you want viewers to think about the teaching team.
- ▶ Make the design recognizable for others to tell what it is.

Name: _____ Date: _____

PRODUCT RUBRIC

Logo Art Installation

	Logo Art Installation	Presentation
Great	Logo is made of 100% recyclable materials, and the combination of materials is unique or creative in some way. Logo clearly captures the essence of the teaching team, depicting the many dimensions that the team has to offer. Installation is a size that best represents its details and can be easily seen from a distance.	All group members speak clearly consistently throughout the presentation; they do not read to audience. Presentation is organized in a professional manner, making it easy to follow. Presentation falls within the 3- to 5-minute range and fulfills the requirements within the timeframe.
Good	Logo is made of 100% recyclable materials, or the combination of materials is unique or creative in some way, but not both. Logo captures the basic message of the teaching team, but only offers a single dimension. Logo is a good size that shows its details but may not be easily seen from a distance.	Group members speak clearly throughout most of the presentation; they read to the audience occasionally. Presentation is organized, making it easy to follow what is being discussed, but it is not as professional as it could be. Presentation falls within the 3- to 5-minute range but does not fulfill all of the requirements within the timeframe.
Needs Improvement	Logo is not made from 100% recyclable materials, and/or it relies on one material for almost all of its construction. Logo does not capture the essence of the teaching team, or the message is very unclear. Logo is either too big or too small.	Group members do not speak clearly; they often read to the audience. Presentation is not organized, making it difficult to follow what is being discussed Presentation does not fall within the 3- to 5-minute range.

2 Focus on Inquiry and Collaboration

Students should be engaging in inquiry on a daily basis. Through inquiry, students discover things for themselves, much like they did when they were young children first learning about their place in the world. Inquiry is what caused them to first discover what got their parents' attention or first emulate another person's actions. Oftentimes the inquiry came from experimenting with something and, if it did not work, learning from mistakes.

The best way to facilitate an environment of inquiry in the classroom is through teaching students to ask the right sorts of questions. Younger students, especially, may need more guidance as to what form these questions will take. And the subject matter students are inquiring about should be rather subjective. If you get into a discussion about what color the sky is, the answer is always going to come down to blue. If, however, you have a more open-ended inquiry, such as what brand of pizza is best or whether it is ever okay to lie, the conversation is going to be endless because there is no correct answer.

Fostering inquiry is what the engineering design process (see Figure 2) is all about. In each and every step, students discover new ideas and concepts for themselves. When they start, they are discovering the problems and constraints by asking questions. They then come up with ideas and a plan, letting their imaginations run wild. The next step involves experimenting with materials and what it will take to make students' ideas come alive. Finally, students look at what they have done and try to make it better, inquiring as to what this might look like.

Part of this process is also having the ability to fail. Failure used to have such a negative connotation in education. Failing a class meant you were not doing well. Now there is a new outlook on failure. Fail actually stands for "first attempt in learning." There should be a space in the classroom where students can make mistakes without fear. This should especially be present during the improve phase of the engineering design process, where students must weigh what has worked, what has not, and figure out how to make the product better. The only way they are going to be able to do this successfully is if they can mess up in the first place.

The ability to work in a group and collaborate is a valuable 21st-century skill that is important to teach, even to young children. Students need to know how to resolve differences with classmates, divvy up tasks amongst peers, and produce something together they would have been unable to produce by themselves. Teachers cannot just put them into groups and hope for the best.

One way to ensure that students are working well together is to give each an individual role that will help the group. This way, instead of five people all trying to take charge, each person has a specific area to specialize in, which will make the quality of the product that much better. If each group member focuses on his or her job, the product the group creates should be better than if any member had worked on it on his or her own. There will likely need to be some conversation about the roles. For example, just making a student the leader might not be enough for him or her to succeed in that role. There might need to be a discussion about what a good leader does. Other roles should also be clearly laid out. If there is room for interpretation, it is best to have a discussion as a class as to what the role should look like.

Once students have been given these roles, there is clear accountability. If something was not written down, it is the scribe who is responsible for it. If a direction was left out of the final product, the quality controller should have caught it. This accountability takes out that mob mentality where everyone in the group is held equally accountable. Even though students are given specific tasks, however, it is important for them to see how collaborating enabled them to develop a better product together.

Hall of Fame

In this project, students will work in groups to create a Hall of Fame for the top 10 accomplishments in science and mathematics. Each group will choose the scientific and mathematical discoveries, theories, and inventions it wishes to induct into its Hall of Fame. As well as what is inducted into the Hall of Fame, students will need to consider the long-term effects of each accomplishment (i.e., the effects of the discovery, invention, etc.) and the reasons for inducting the accomplishment into their Hall of Fame. At the end of the project, groups will present their Hall of Fame and an exhibition of their top three inductees.

Materials

- Project Outline: Hall of Fame (student copies)
- Suggested Timeline
- Lesson: What Is a Hall of Fame?
- Handout 2.1: Hall of Fame Brainstorm (student copies)
- Handout 2.2: Developing Your Exhibition and Presentation (student copies)
- Product Rubric: Hall of Fame (student copies)

PROJECT OUTLINE

Hall of Fame

Big Idea

There are many great scientific and mathematical accomplishments.

Essential Question

How can you rate the top 10 accomplishments in science and mathematics?

Deliverables

You will work in a group to create a Hall of Fame for the top 10 accomplishments in science and mathematics. You and your group members will choose the scientific and mathematical discoveries, theories, and inventions you wish to induct into your Hall of Fame. You will also need to consider the long-term effects of each accomplishment (i.e., the effects of the discovery, invention, etc.) and the reasons for inducting the accomplishment into your Hall of Fame. At the end of the project, you will present your Hall of Fame and an exhibition of your top three inductees.

Members of your group will take on the following roles:

▸ **Team Lead:** Responsible for keeping the group on task and making sure that group members fulfill their roles.

▸ **Cross Checker:** Responsible for checking the research the group uses to make sure information is accurate and from reliable sources.

▸ **Curator:** Responsible for the display of the exhibition of the top three inductees.

▸ **Spokesperson:** Responsible for acting as the primary speaker in the final presentation.

Constraints

Your project will be graded on three criteria:

▸ presentation,

▸ content, and

▸ display.

Bonus Opportunities

Design the building/make a model of where the Hall of Fame will be housed based on science and mathematical concepts.

SUGGESTED TIMELINE

DAY				
1 Introduce the project and conduct Lesson: What Is a Hall of Fame? *Ask.*	**2** Divide students into groups to begin brainstorming (see Handout 2.1). *Ask.*	**3** Have groups brainstorm ideas. *Imagine.*	**4** Have groups research scientific and mathematical accomplishments. *Plan.*	**5** Have groups research scientific and mathematical accomplishments. *Plan.*
6 Have groups research scientific and mathematical accomplishments. *Plan.*	**7** Have groups narrow down their lists of accomplishments. *Plan.*	**8** Have groups decide on their top three accomplishments. *Imagine.*	**9** Have groups create their displays for their top three accomplishments. *Create.*	**10** Have groups create their displays for their top three accomplishments. *Create.*
11 Have groups create their displays for their top three accomplishments. *Create.*	**12** Have groups develop their presentations (see Handout 2.2). *Plan.*	**13** Have groups develop their presentations. *Create.*	**14** Have groups practice their presentations. *Improve.*	**15** Have groups present their Halls of Fame.

LESSON

What Is a Hall of Fame?

1. Ask students: *When you think about a Hall of Fame, what do you think of?* Guide students to understand that a Hall of Fame houses the best of the best, legends, long-lasting accomplishments, innovations, and game changers.

2. Explain that the famous Baseball Hall of Fame has 323 inductees. This may seem like a lot, but one has to consider that baseball has been played since the 1800s and more than 20,000 people have played Major League Baseball. In other words, just a small percentage of players make it into the Hall of Fame.

3. Ask students to create a class Hall of Fame for a topic they are familiar with (e.g., cartoons):

   ▶ Have students set criteria for entering the Hall of Fame (e.g., the inductee must have been an animated television show, aired for at least three seasons, aired 10 years ago or more, and be well-known in popular culture).

   ▶ Have students select contenders (e.g., *The Bugs Bunny Show*, *Tom and Jerry*, *The Flintstones*, *The Simpsons*, *SpongeBob SquarePants*, *Scooby-Doo, Where Are You!*, etc.).

   ▶ Have students keep in mind possible rejections from the Hall of Fame and why they may not be contenders (e.g., *Gravity Falls* was too recent and only ran for two seasons, *The Wiggles* is not fully animated, etc.).

Name: _____ Date: _____

Hall of Fame Brainstorm

Directions: Working on your own, develop your own list of 10 potential nominations to your group's Hall of Fame. Use this handout to organize your research. When all of your group members have developed lists of nominations, compare your lists and work together to narrow down your nominees.

1. Accomplishment: _____
   ▸ Why is this scientific or mathematical accomplishment important?

   ▸ What are the long-term effects of this accomplishment?

2. Accomplishment: _____
   ▸ Why is this scientific or mathematical accomplishment important?

   ▸ What are the long-term effects of this accomplishment?

3. Accomplishment: _____
   ▸ Why is this scientific or mathematical accomplishment important?

   ▸ What are the long-term effects of this accomplishment?

Project 2: Focus on Inquiry and Collaboration

Handout 2.1: Hall of Fame Brainstorm, *continued*

4. Accomplishment: _____
   ▸ Why is this scientific or mathematical accomplishment important?

   ▸ What are the long-term effects of this accomplishment?

5. Accomplishment: _____
   ▸ Why is this scientific or mathematical accomplishment important?

   ▸ What are the long-term effects of this accomplishment?

6. Accomplishment: _____
   ▸ Why is this scientific or mathematical accomplishment important?

   ▸ What are the long-term effects of this accomplishment?

7. Accomplishment: _____
   ▸ Why is this scientific or mathematical accomplishment important?

   ▸ What are the long-term effects of this accomplishment?

Project 2: Focus on Inquiry and Collaboration

Name: _____ Date: _____

Handout 2.1: Hall of Fame Brainstorm, *continued*

8. Accomplishment: _____
   - ▸ Why is this scientific or mathematical accomplishment important?

   - ▸ What are the long-term effects of this accomplishment?

9. Accomplishment: _____
   - ▸ Why is this scientific or mathematical accomplishment important?

   - ▸ What are the long-term effects of this accomplishment?

10. Accomplishment: _____
    - ▸ Why is this scientific or mathematical accomplishment important?

    - ▸ What are the long-term effects of this accomplishment?

Name: _____   Date: _____

HANDOUT 2.2

Developing Your Exhibition and Presentation

Directions: The following tips and resources will be useful to you as you develop your exhibitions and your presentation.

Tips for Creating a Display

- A good display is easy to see and understand.
- A good display is informative but does not include too much detail.
- A good display looks professional.
- Visit some Hall of Fame websites and look at their displays, such as the Pro Football Hall of Fame (http://www.profootballhof.com), the Rock and Roll Hall of Fame (https://www.rockhall.com), the National Baseball Hall of Fame (https://baseball hall.org), or the National Inventors Hall of Fame (http://www.invent.org).

Tips for Developing Your Presentation

You will have no more than 10 minutes to present your proposal for the Hall of Fame. You must include:

- Your list of 10 nominees.
- The exhibition display for your top 3 nominees.
- Your rationale for your decisions. Remember, you are trying to convince people why your choices are the best.

When presenting, there are some things to consider:

- Do you speak at a pace that allows others to understand?
- Do you speak loud enough for people to hear?
- Do you avoid crossing your arms or sticking your hands in your pockets while speaking?
- Do you make occasional eye contact with the audience?
- Do you present rather than read?
- Do you refer to your visuals?
- Do you have a clear beginning, middle, and end to your presentation?
- Do you use examples and detail to make your points stronger?

Project 2: Focus on Inquiry and Collaboration

Name: _____ Date: _____

PRODUCT RUBRIC

Hall of Fame

	Content	Presentation	Display
Excellent	Group includes many details and examples to defend choices. Group makes a clear argument for why each nominee should be considered for the Hall of Fame. Group shows the long-term effects of all of the accomplishments.	Speakers present clearly consistently throughout; they do not read to audience. Students choose 10 solid nominees to submit to the Hall of Fame. Presentation is organized in a professional manner, making it easy to follow.	Display looks professional, like something that would be on display in a museum. Display clearly captures the three accomplishments. Display is easy for people to view and shows many details.
Good	Group includes details and examples to defend choices, but the arguments could be clearer. Group makes an argument for why most of the items should be considered for the Hall of Fame but not all 10. Group shows the long-term effects of most of the accomplishments but not all.	Speakers present clearly most of the time; they read to audience occasionally. Students choose 10 nominees to submit to the Hall of Fame, but not all are strong choices. Presentation is organized, but it is not as professional as it could be.	Display looks somewhat professional, like a high-quality school project. Display captures the three accomplishments, but a few important details are left out. Display and its details can be viewed, but some details are difficult to see.

Name: _____ Date: _____

Product Rubric: Hall of Fame, *continued*

	Content	Presentation	Display
Needs Improvement	Group includes few or no details and examples to defend choices. Group makes a clumsy argument for why each accomplishment should be considered for the Hall of Fame. Group does not show the long-term effects of many of the accomplishments.	Speakers do not present clearly; they often read to the audience. Students choose fewer than 10 nominees to submit to the Hall of Fame. Presentation is not organized, making it difficult to follow.	Display does not look professional. Display does not capture three accomplishments in any way. Display is not easy for people to view, leaving out many details about the three accomplishments.

10 Performance-Based STEM Projects for Grades 6–8 © Prufrock Press Inc.

3 Understand Multiple Content Areas

Once in the real world, students have to be able to pull different skills learned in separate arenas and put them together. Different subjects and skills work together to get desired results. What if schools facilitated more opportunities for students to build crosscurricular skills? STEM education is a perfect example of combining subject areas. Many educators include art in STEM education, known as STEAM. Others, still, include reading (STREAM), as there are connections to English language arts and literacy across the curriculum, such as writing a research paper, reading for comprehension, or conducting an interview. The sooner you expose students to a crosscurricular model, the better, as crosscurricular learning results in more authentic learning. Through crosscurricular lessons and activities, students can better understand the context of what they are learning and how it fits into the real world.

You know crosscurricular learning is working when students are utilizing skills from various subject areas—perhaps without even realizing the connections at first. If students are writing a research paper on the importance of various modes of transportation, such as the railroad, steamboats, and national roads, they may not realize they are learning about history while doing so or, alternatively, might not realize they are using language arts skills to learn about history. Or, during a science project involving the creation of a new version of a mousetrap, students may not realize the math skills they are developing by drawing a plan with dimensions.

The advantages to this integrated learning for students are many. A comprehensive study on "The Logic of Interdisciplinary Studies" (Mathison & Feeman, 1997) discovered that students experienced:

- an increase in understanding, retention, and application of general concepts;
- a better overall comprehension of global interdependencies, along with the development of multiple perspectives, points of view, and values;
- an increase in the ability to make decisions, think critically and creatively, and synthesize knowledge beyond the disciplines;
- the increased ability to identify, assess and transfer significant information needed for solving novel problems;
- the promotion of cooperative learning, a better attitude toward the self as a learner and as a meaningful member of a community; and
- increased motivation (pp. 19–20).

Integrated approaches make learning more organic and less forced. As human beings we are natural learners. From the moment we are born, we are learning every single second through experience. And yet, in school, we often take these experiences away and try to make what is being taught rigid and artificial. By using integrated learning, we allow students to experience how these subject areas all work together in the natural order of things. When learning is more natural, so are the results.

You Be the Teacher

In this project, students will determine a STEM topic they wish to teach the rest of the class about and develop a lesson plan. Students may work individually, with partners, or in groups. The topic must be something that others will find useful, and students must already be experts on the topic or become experts on it. Students may include a presentation, worksheets, projects, and even a test in their lesson for students to complete. Students must develop a learning goal and determine a way to assess whether or not other students have mastered the goal.

Materials

- ▶ Project Outline: You Be the Teacher (student copies)
- ▶ Suggested Timeline
- ▶ Lesson: Effective Teaching
- ▶ Handout 3.1: Selecting a Topic (student copies)
- ▶ Handout 3.2: Lesson Planning (student copies)
- ▶ Handout 3.3: Creating Your Assessment (student copies)
- ▶ Handout 3.4: Improving Your Lesson (student copies)
- ▶ Product Rubric: You Be the Teacher (student copies)

PROJECT OUTLINE

You Be the Teacher

Big Idea

Teaching can be a valuable learning tool.

Essential Question

How do you craft an effective lesson?

Deliverables

You will determine a topic that you wish to teach the rest of the class about and develop a lesson plan. You may include a presentation, worksheets, projects, and even a test in your lesson for other students to complete. You must develop a learning goal and determine a way to assess whether or not other students have mastered the goal.

Constraints

Your lesson must:
▸ be at least 10 minutes long but no longer than 30 minutes,
▸ be tied to a learning goal, and
▸ include a way to assess student mastery.

SUGGESTED TIMELINE

DAY				
1 Introduce the project and conduct Lesson: Effective Teaching. *Ask.*	**2** Have students select topics (see Handout 3.1). *Imagine.*	**3** Have students plan their lessons (see Handout 3.2). *Plan.*	**4** Have students plan their lessons. *Plan.*	**5** Have students create their lessons. *Create.*
6 Have students create their lessons. *Create.*	**7** Have students create their assessments (see Handout 3.3). *Create.*	**8** Have students create their assessments. *Create.*	**9** Have students practice their lessons (see Handout 3.4). *Improve.*	**10** Have students revise their lessons based on the rubric and student feedback. *Improve.*
11 Have students present lessons.	**12** Have students present lessons.	**13** Have students present lessons.	**14** Have students present lessons.	**15** Have students present lessons.

LESSON

Effective Teaching

1. Ask students: *What are qualities of good lessons that you have experienced?* Elicit responses. Guide students to understand that effective lessons are fun, engaging, hands-on, clear, and organized.

2. Ask: *What are qualities of poor lessons?* Elicit responses. Guide students to understand that ineffective lessons may involve students being talked at, are boring, are confusing, or involve too much busy work.

3. Ask: *What are some techniques that teachers use that seem useful to you?* Students may suggest strategies such as involving students, repeating important things, making real-world connections, including visuals, or including a hands-on component, game, or competition to learn content.

HANDOUT 3.1

Selecting a Topic

Directions: When choosing a topic there are several different things to consider:
- ▸ Are you knowledgeable about the topic?
- ▸ Is the topic something that can be taught in less than a half hour?
- ▸ Is the topic something you would be excited about teaching?
- ▸ Is the topic something you realistically can teach at school?
- ▸ Is the topic something appropriate for school?

Tips for Brainstorming Topic Ideas

1. Write down 10 things that you would be interested in teaching others.

2. Compare these with the things to consider in the list above.

3. Are there any topics that you eliminated?

4. Out of the topics left, which one would be the:
    - ▸ easiest to plan,
    - ▸ the most fun,
    - ▸ the most useful,
    - ▸ the coolest, and/or
    - ▸ the most challenging?

Project 3: Understand Multiple Content Areas

Handout 3.1: Selecting a Topic, *continued*

5. Decide for yourself out of the descriptions in Question 4, which one(s) are the most important to you.

6. If you have a single topic that fits the criteria for what is required and what meets your own criteria, then you should probably pick that one.

7. If you still have a few to choose from, consider a couple of ideas for tiebreakers:
   ▸ Ask some friends for their opinion.
   ▸ Poll a few classmates about which topic they would be most interested in.
   ▸ Ask the teacher which topic he or she thinks would be the better choice.
   ▸ See if someone else is covering a certain topic. You don't want two lessons on the same topic.
   ▸ If all else fails, flip a coin or have someone randomly pick.

HANDOUT 3.2

Lesson Planning

Directions: Once you have chosen your topic, there are several things to consider:

- ▸ How will you assess whether students have mastered the skill or not? (You can decide when to assess for mastery. For example, you can have students complete a test at the end of the lesson or a demonstration during the middle of the lesson.)
- ▸ What sort of materials or equipment will you need to gather?
- ▸ What will be the best way to approach teaching students about this topic (e.g., hands-on activity, lecture, group work, demonstration)?
- ▸ What will students need to do in order to demonstrate mastery?
- ▸ What skills do you have to learn in order to teach others about the topic (i.e., how to make a PowerPoint, perform a certain task, demonstrate a certain lesson)?

Also consider the beginning, middle, and end of your lesson. What will those look like, and how much time will be spent on each of them?

- ▸ **Beginning:** Typically an introduction to the topic.
- ▸ **Middle:** The meat of the lesson where students are exposed to the topic and get to see it for themselves.
- ▸ **End:** A wrap-up of the lesson, including what the main takeaways were and the answering of any questions for clarity.

Use the graphic organizer to plan your lesson.

Lesson Plan

Topic: _____

Learning Goal: _____

_____

_____

_____

Project 3: Understand Multiple Content Areas

Name: _____ Date: _____

Other Skills Learned

▸

▸

▸

▸

How Will You Organize the Lesson?

Beginning: _____

Middle: _____

End: _____

What materials are needed for the lesson? _____

_____

_____

How will you assess mastery of what was taught? _____

_____

_____

Student Signature: _____

Teacher Signature: _____

Name: _____ Date: _____

HANDOUT 3.3

Creating Your Assessment

Directions: As a teacher, you need to determine if students mastered your lesson. You can check for student mastery through an assessment.

An assessment does not need to be a pencil-and-paper test or worksheet. There are many other ways for students to show mastery, such as:

- developing a a product,
- conducting a demonstration,
- through teacher observation,
- homework,
- group work, and/or
- success or failure at a task.

During a lesson, when you give the assessment is always dependent on where mastery would best be evaluated. Often times this is at the end of the lesson, but it does not have to be. Consider when and what would be best for students to be able to show mastery of your lesson.

Name: _____ Date: _____

Improving Your Lesson

Directions: One of the most difficult things about teaching a lesson is time management. Something you think is going to take 5 minutes may end up taking 20 minutes, or something you think is going to last 15 minutes may only take a couple of minutes.

In order to make sure this doesn't happen, you are going to find a partner or two and present your lesson in its entirety.

In addition to timing the lesson, your partner(s) should also answer the following questions for you:

1. Was it clear what was being taught during the lesson?

2. Was the lesson organized?

3. Did the lesson have all of the necessary materials needed?

4. Did the assessment given show mastery of what students were supposed to learn?

5. Was the speaker loud and clear enough?

Name: _____ Date: _____

PRODUCT RUBRIC

You Be the Teacher

	Lesson Organization	Lesson Content	Assessment
Excellent	Lesson is organized in a professional manner; it has a clear beginning, middle, and end, making it easy to follow. Lesson makes excellent use of time; it is 10–30 minutes long and covers all of the important learning goals. Teacher(s) has all of the necessary materials needed to teach the lesson and distributes them in an orderly fashion.	Learning goals are clearly laid out and referred to throughout the course of the lesson. Lesson's format is meaningful to the content being presented, adding to students' understanding. Lesson covers more than just the basics; it takes students to a deeper level of understanding.	Assessment evaluates whether students truly gained mastery of the topic. Assessment allows for the teacher(s) to truly assess mastery of the learning goals. Assessment is objective; it has clear criteria for how it is evaluated.
Good	Lesson is organized, having a beginning, middle, and end, but it is not always easy to follow. Lesson makes good use of time; it is 10–30 minutes long, but not all of the learning goals are covered. Teacher(s) has all of the necessary materials needed to teach the lesson, although some time is wasted in how they are distributed.	Learning goals are mentioned and referred to occasionally, but they are not focused on enough. Lesson's format is appropriate to the content being presented, providing a basic vehicle for the lesson. Lesson covers the basics; it does not take students to a deeper level of understanding.	Assessment evaluates whether students gained a basic understanding of the topic but not full mastery. Assessment's format allows for the teacher(s) to assess what students learned, but it does not show whether mastery was gained. Assessment is mostly objective; it has clear criteria for how it is evaluated, but there are parts where opinion counts more than actual skills.

Project 3: Understand Multiple Content Areas

Product Rubric: You Be the Teacher, *continued*

	Lesson Organization	Lesson Content	Assessment
Needs Improvement	Lesson is not organized; it is difficult to tell what is the beginning, middle, and/or end. Lesson does not make good use of time; it is longer or shorter than 10–30 minutes, and it does not cover all of the important learning goals. Teacher(s) does not have all of the necessary materials needed to teach the lesson.	Learning goals are not mentioned or are not referred to throughout the lesson. Lesson's format is not appropriate to the content presented. Lesson does not cover the basics; many important details are left out.	Assessment does not evaluate whether students gained any understanding of the topic. Assessment's format does not allow for the teacher(s) to assess what students learned. Assessment is mostly subjective.

4 Explore Contemporary Issues

Students learn reading, writing, and arithmetic, but we also hope that they will learn to be better people during their time in school. This starts by having awareness—first of those immediately around them. We can grow students' awareness by teaching them to be polite and considerate of their classmates, teachers, and other school community staff through character education. Then, this immediate environment can be expanded to include the community that they live in. What are the town's problems? What can students do to help or contribute more to their community? This grows and grows, expanding to their country and then, ideally, to global awareness.

Global awareness means more than being aware of current events going on around the world. According to the Partnership for 21st Century Skills (2016), global awareness entails:

- ▸ Using 21st century skills to understand and address global issues
- ▸ Learning from and working collaboratively with individuals representing diverse cultures, religions and lifestyles in a spirit of mutual respect and open dialogue in personal, work and community contexts

▸ Understanding other nations and cultures, including the use of non-English languages (p. 2)

Global awareness helps students to understand and appreciate personal and social context. Personal context refers to the intrapersonal environment that shapes an individual's experience. Such environmental factors play a role in determining the student's response to experiences and interactions. If a person is prejudiced against someone else or another group or culture, it is probably due to an experience or something that was relayed to him or her that caused such a response. People do not choose to be prejudiced; rather their intrapersonal environment often shapes them into being that way. Social context is recognizing that sometimes your own personal context and that of those around you are not necessarily the same. As an example, this has come up in the news recently: Personal tweets authored by public figures many years ago when they were younger and less aware of the social context of their comments are coming to light, and these individuals are now facing the repercussions. The lesson here is that your digital footprint is there forever. A comment you once made might have been fine in the personal context of your friends, but once exposed to the public, it can come back to haunt you.

To help students become more aware, expose them to contemporary issues that society is dealing with. This could be something that is happening in your town, a cause that needs support, or a worldwide problem, such as hunger or lack of an education. Showing students that they can make a difference can have an effect on their personal context. They might see something from another point of view or gain an understanding of something they were previously ignorant about.

Community service projects are an excellent way for students to learn about contemporary issues, as well as use the engineering design process to problem solve. Whether gathering canned foods for the local pantry, educating others about the opioid epidemic, raising money for kids with cancer, or trying to create practical solutions for farming in third-world countries, students will gain an awareness of the people in these situations and develop empathy. One thing that can frustrate students, especially younger ones, is feeling like there is nothing they can do about a problem. They hear about children starving in Africa, hurricanes that devastate Puerto Rico, or the homeless people in their town, and empathize with the people who are affected. Helping students to understand how they can help not only makes them aware of the problem, but it also makes them aware of what can be done about it.

The Role of Citizenship

In this project, students will create a community service project to better either the school or the community around them. In order to first introduce students to community service, host a Community Service Speakers Fair, in which you invite speakers from various nonprofit organizations to speak to students about what they do to help others. Depending on your class, grade, or school size, you may invite one, two, or more speakers. Students can choose which speakers they listen to, or you can have students rotate between speakers. Visit http://www.nonprofitlist.org to locate nonprofit organizations near you, or consider organizations such as your local food pantry or soup kitchen, a local animal shelter, a local senior center, Amnesty International, the American Red Cross, Toys for Tots, the Salvation Army, etc.

Provide students with one week to set up their projects and 3 weeks to conduct their projects. Approve students' topics. As they plan, students will need to research their topics and/or make phone calls or e-mails to members of the public or local nonprofit organizations. Throughout the project, students should collect evidence of their project (e.g., photos, letters from those they helped, and/or video) and seek to conduct a project with long-term results. Students should also stay on task and work independently as much as possible.

Periodically check in with students. Request that students provide you with a contact number for any places and people they are working with and call to make sure everything is going well. For a project where students are doing much of the work independently, it is important to check in on their progress. Consider meeting with students once a week to get an idea of how their projects are progressing. During this conversation, you might want to ask (some questions may not apply depending on a student's project):

▸ Have you started your community service project? If not, when are you planning to begin?

▸ Have you run into any obstacles in doing your community service project? What do you think might be some ways around [the obstacle]?

▸ Are you enjoying your community service project? If not, is there anything that could be changed to make it more enjoyable?

▸ Have you made arrangements with the organization you are working with to drop off items you have collected?

▸ How much more do you need to work on your community service project? What is your plan?

▸ Will you have enough time to complete the project in 3 weeks? If you think you will not, how are you going to adjust?

▸ Do you think you will continue your project once the assignment is over?

At the end of the project, have students reflect on their work (see Handout 4.3).

Materials

▸ Project Outline: The Role of Citizenship (student copies)
▸ Suggested Timeline
▸ Handout 4.1: Choosing Your Topic (student copies)
▸ Handout 4.2: Contacting Others (student copies)
▸ Handout 4.3: Reflection (student copies)
▸ Product Rubric: The Role of Citizenship (student copies)

Name: _____ Date: _____

PROJECT OUTLINE

The Role of Citizenship

Big Idea

An important aspect of citizenship is helping the community.

Essential Question

What can you do to help your community?

Deliverables

You will create a community service project to better either your school or the community around you. You will have one week to set up your project and 3 weeks to conduct your project. You must first have your teacher approve your topic. Then, as you plan your project, you will need to research your topic and/or make phone calls or e-mails to members of the public or local nonprofit organizations. Throughout the project, you should collect evidence of your project (e.g., photos, letters from those you helped, and/or video) and seek to conduct a project with long-term results. You should also stay on task and work independently as much as possible.

Constraints

Your project must be completed within 3 weeks, and you cannot be paid or compensated for the work that you do.

SUGGESTED TIMELINE

DAY				
1 Introduce the project and host a Community Service Speakers Fair. *Ask.*	**2** Have students brainstorm ideas for their community service projects (see Handout 4.1). *Imagine.*	**3** Have students research ideas for their community service projects (see Handout 4.2). *Plan.*	**4** Have students research ideas for their community service projects. *Plan.*	**5** Have students decide on their ideas. *Plan.*
6 Have students conduct their community service projects. *Create.*	**7** Have students conduct their community service projects. *Create.*	**8** Have students conduct their community service projects. *Create.*	**9** Have students conduct their community service projects. *Create.*	**10** Meet with students to check in on progress. *Improve.*
11 Have students conduct their community service projects. *Create.*	**12** Have students conduct their community service projects. *Create.*	**13** Have students conduct their community service projects. *Create.*	**14** Have students conduct their community service projects. *Create.*	**15** Meet with students to check in on progress. *Improve.*
16 Have students conduct their community service projects. *Create.*	**17** Have students conduct their community service projects. *Create.*	**18** Have students conduct their community service projects. *Create.*	**19** Have students complete their community service projects. *Create.*	**20** Have students reflect on their work (see Handout 4.3).

10 Performance-Based STEM Projects for Grades 6–8 © Prufrock Press Inc.

HANDOUT 4.1

Choosing Your Topic

Directions: There are many things that you can do in order to better your community. With only one week to set up your project and 3 weeks to conduct your project, you want to make sure that your project is both meaningful and able to be completed within the time frame. The following lists are provided to offer you some guidance. But get creative! These lists are not exhaustive.

Meaningful Service Projects

▶ Collecting canned goods for the local shelter from a large group of people (school, church, sports team)
▶ Volunteering in a retirement community
▶ Picking up trash at the local park
▶ Tutoring a student
▶ Raising money for a good cause (e.g., breast cancer research, diabetes awareness)
▶ Educating others on issues affecting the community
▶ Adopting a needy family during the holidays
▶ Putting together packages for soldiers overseas
▶ Teaching sports to a group of younger children
▶ Starting a community garden

Not-So-Meaningful Service Projects

▶ Doing chores around the house
▶ Helping a neighbor one time
▶ Picking up trash in your own yard
▶ Donating just your own money to a cause
▶ Tutoring a brother or sister
▶ Babysitting

Service Projects to Avoid

▶ Working at a hospital, zoo, or animal shelter (usually takes too long to set up)
▶ Anything you get paid for
▶ Something that was going to be done anyway (e.g., your church was already collecting trash, and you helped)
▶ Fund raiser sponsored by someone else (e.g., a walk-a-thon)
▶ Things that only help your family

HANDOUT 4.2

Contacting Others

Directions: When you call or e-mail to discuss doing community service, remember a few things:

- ▸ Make sure you state the purpose of your phone call or e-mail.
- ▸ Be sure to provide your name and phone number/e-mail (if you are leaving a message, make sure you do this twice).
- ▸ Prepare some of the questions ahead of time, such as:
  - ▹ Do you have volunteer opportunities during the time I'm doing this project?
  - ▹ Is there an age restriction?
  - ▹ Do I need to complete any training?

- ▸ Remember that the person you are contacting is doing you a favor, so be respectful of his or her time and effort.
- ▸ You may have to talk to several people before you get a hold of the person you are looking for.
- ▸ If someone does not seem like the person you need to be talking to, make sure you ask him or her who you should be talking with. Get a name and contact information.
- ▸ If you leave a voicemail or e-mail, make sure you follow up after a couple of days.
- ▸ Even though you are younger, you can still act in a professional manner at all times.

Name: _____ Date: _____

HANDOUT 4.3
Reflection

Directions: Consider what you learned during your community service project and answer the following questions.

1. What do you think was successful in your community service project?

2. What could have been done better in your community service project?

3. When it came to the management of your time, do you think you paced yourself well, or were there things you might have managed better?

4. If you had to do your project over again, what would you do differently?

Handout 4.3: Reflection, *continued*

5. If you were to give someone advice if he or she was doing a similar project, what would you tell him or her?

6. Do you think your project had an impact on the community?

7. How could a project such as this be done on a larger scale?

8. Consider other students' projects. Which one do you think would have a large impact on the community?

Name: _____ Date: _____

PRODUCT RUBRIC

The Role of Citizenship

	Service Project	Responsibility
Great	Student has multiple forms of evidence of his or her project (e.g., photos, letters from those helped, and/or video). Student conducted a service project with long-term results. Student is able to convey meaningfully how his or her project helped the community.	Student completed the service project on time and worked additionally on the project, extending it beyond the assignment. Student stayed on task throughout the project, showing specific evidence whenever conferencing with the teacher. Student was able to act independently on the project without intervention from the teacher.
Good	Student has evidence of his or her project but only in a single form (e.g., photos, letters from those helped, or video). Student conducts a successful service project, but the results are short-term and at a surface level. Student is able to convey how his or her project helped the community but without much meaning.	Student completed the service project on time. Student stayed mostly on task throughout the project, showing specific evidence whenever conferencing with the teacher. Student was mostly able to act independently on the project, but occasionally needed intervention from the teacher.
Needs Improvement	Student does not have evidence of his or her project. Student did not conduct a successful service project, letting obstacles and roadblocks stop him or her from moving forward. Student is not able to convey how his or her project helped the community.	Student was not able to complete the project on time. Student did not stay on task throughout the project, or could not provide any specific evidence whenever conferencing with the teacher. Student was not able to act independently on the project, needing much intervention from the teacher.

5 Use Technology, Math, and Reasoning

Abstract reasoning can be a challenge for students, especially younger ones. This is because they think very much in concrete terms; this or that, black or white, wrong or right. What does it mean to be an abstract thinker? An abstract thinker:

- ▶ can understand and separate context from content;
- ▶ is able to understand relationships between events or can connect the dots;
- ▶ understands the meaning behind words, situations, and events;
- ▶ draws generalizations from a specific set of circumstances; and
- ▶ has the ability to compare different situations.

According to Stanley (2018), you might hear an abstract thinker "say, 'I wonder . . .' or 'What if this happened . . . ?' They are able to think about situations that are not there, but other students may only be able to think about what is right in front of them" (p. 173). In the classroom, abstract thinkers:

- ▶ are able to use metaphors and analogies with ease;
- ▶ can understand the relationship between both verbal and nonverbal ideas;

> ▸ possess complex reasoning skills, such as critical thinking and problem solving;
> ▸ can mentally maneuver objects without having to physically do it, known as spatial reasoning;
> ▸ are adept at imagining situations that have happened or are not actually happening; and
> ▸ appreciate sarcasm. (p. 173)

Math has a lot of abstract thinking. Even the act of learning to count has many abstract qualities to it, such as (Scholastic, n.d.):

> ▸ **The stable-order rule:** Saying counting words only once and in a consistent order (e.g., "seven, eight, nine . . .").
> ▸ **The cardinal rule:** Giving a summary or "how many" total. When starting out, children might have to recount to remember the total, but they eventually learn that the last number counted represents the whole, an abstract concept.
> ▸ **The abstraction rule:** Not just numbers can be counted. Any object can be counted, whether it be the number of times bouncing a ball, the number of stuffed animals a child owns, etc. You can also count the lack of an object. If you have a tennis ball can with only two balls in it, you can count the missing ball as one.

Not all students naturally think abstractly. But how do we get them to do so using technology and math? One way to do this is through the use of manipulatives. Manipulatives are "items you can touch and move around that allow a student to count, figure out fractions, discern patterns, and other math tasks" (Stanley, 2018, p. 176). Manipulatives include blocks, shapes, base ten blocks, Unifix cubes, fraction bars, and plastic counting cubes. You can also use technology to create manipulatives. There are several digital manipulatives available for students, such as ST Math, which often requires students to manipulate objects in order to arrive at the correct answer, or visual manipulatives like tangrams, which represent physical objects.

Helping students to think abstractly, or develop outside-the-box thinking, will lead to more creativity and innovation. After all, anyone who thinks inside the box can only produce what is in that box. Those who are thinking outside of it can develop new ideas.

What If You Paid the Bills?

In this project, students will explore maintaining a monthly budget. Students will be assigned a salary and required to rent an apartment, purchase groceries and other necessities, pay bills, and see if they can stay under budget. You can assign students jobs randomly or provide students with a choice related to their career interests. Students also might want to consider specific cities for specific careers. In other words, if they want to be an actor, they might have to live in Los Angeles or New York. Or if they want to be a marine biologist, they probably need a city near an ocean.

You can determine students' salaries or have students determine their salaries by researching average salaries, such as via the list available at https://www.payscale.com/salaries-by-occupation or https://www.bls.gov/oes/current/oes_nat.htm.

Throughout the course of the project, students can randomly draw life cards (see Handout 5.4). These life cards include surprise scenarios. Some of these scenarios are positive developments; others are not. Students must adjust their budgets according to these life cards. You might consider adding life cards pertinent to your students. You will need to determine how often and how many life cards are drawn at once, as well as whether you will have students draw cards individually or as a class (i.e., whether the scenario affects one student or all students).

At the end of the project, you can consider having students' parents or guardians review the product rubric and grade their students' work.

Materials

- ▶ Project Outline: What If You Paid the Bills? (student copies)
- ▶ Suggested Timeline
- ▶ Lesson: Budget Simulation
- ▶ Lesson: Budget Overview
- ▶ Handout 5.1: Budget Simulation Worksheet (student copies)
- ▶ Handout 5.2: Criteria for Portfolio (student copies)
- ▶ Handout 5.3: Researching for Your Portfolio (student copies)
- ▶ Handout 5.4: Life Cards (cut out in advance)
- ▶ Product Rubric: What If You Paid the Bills? (student copies)

PROJECT OUTLINE

What If You Paid the Bills?

Big Idea

Budgeting is an important financial tool.

Essential Question

How can you develop an accurate and effective budget?

Deliverables

You will explore maintaining a monthly budget. You will be assigned a salary and required to rent an apartment, purchase groceries and other necessities, pay bills, and see if you can stay under budget. You will collect your information in a portfolio. You will have to balance your budget at the end of the month to see if you have been successful.

Your portfolio will be graded on a few criteria:

▶ Is it accurate? Do the figures and estimates in the portfolio seem realistic and researched?

▶ Is it organized? Can someone flip through and tell what each page is trying to communicate, either through labels, headings, or being very clear in your opening sentences?

▶ Is it complete? Does your portfolio meet all of the requirements?

▶ Does it have a rationale? Do you explain why you made the decisions that you made?

▶ Does it have details and examples? The more detail and examples you use, the clearer your explanation is going to be. Provide the reader with a clear picture of what you are trying to explain.

Constraints

You must budget for the entire month, and you cannot rely on outside sources of income.

SUGGESTED TIMELINE

DAY				
1 Introduce the project and conduct Lesson: Budget Simulation. *Ask.*	**2** Conduct Lesson: Budget Overview. *Ask.*	**3** Assign student jobs and salaries and have students choose the cities they live in. *Imagine.*	**4** Have students research for their portfolios (see Handout 5.2 and Handout 5.3). *Plan.*	**5** Have students research for their portfolios. *Plan.*
6 Have students research for their portfolios. *Plan.*	**7** Have students research for their portfolios. *Plan.*	**8** Have students research for their portfolios. *Plan.*	**9** Have students research for their portfolios. *Plan.*	**10** Have students prepare their portfolios (Part A). *Create.*
11 Have students prepare their portfolios (Part B). *Create.*	**12** Have students prepare their portfolios (Part C). *Create.*	**13** Have students prepare their portfolios (Part D). *Create.*	**14** Have students balance their budgets and make any adjustments. *Improve.*	**15** Have students' parents review the product rubric and grade students' work.

LESSON

Budget Simulation

1. Have students practice a mini-budget activity. Have students play the game Careers, in which they are assigned a salary and must go through life experiences, and/or have students run through a simple grocery store simulation, outlined in the following steps.

2. Tell students that they have $200 to buy enough groceries to last them the entire month. This includes food, drinks, and anything else they might consume at a meal. Students will not be eating out at restaurants. Distribute Handout 5.1 for students to complete as they work through the simulation.

3. Explain that students will first want to determine how many meals they are going to have. If they eat breakfast, lunch, and dinner each day for a month, that would be 30 days x 3 meals, which would equal 90 meals.

4. Explain: *You are going to generate a list of groceries that you are going to buy, keeping a running tally on how much you have spent. You will need to determine if you have enough food to eat for the month, and, if not, you will need to make adjustments to your grocery list.*

5. You can either have students look up prices at local grocery stores online, or use the following link, which has a good collection of goods and their prices: https://h2savecom.files.wordpress.com/2015/02/hip-price-list-sheet1.pdf.

Budget Overview

1. Distribute Handout 5.2 and explain that students will need to research most of the criteria for their portfolios.
2. Walk through some examples of the criteria for the portfolio, as needed:
   - **Housing:** A one-bedroom apartment might cost $500 to $3,600 a month. A security deposit might be a percentage of one month's rent or cost up to two months' rent.
   - **Utilities:** Utilities might include electricity, phone, gas, water, trash, etc. Students should see if their apartment complex or landlord covers some or all utilities.
   - **Renter's insurance:** Renter's insurance might cost $100 to $300 a year.
   - **Transportation:** A car might cost $3,000 to $15,000 (of course, this depends on a student's salary and how much they wish to spend on a vehicle). Auto insurance might cost $100 to $200 a month. Car repairs usually correlate with how old the vehicle is or how many miles are on the vehicle. For gas, students might estimate 1,000 miles a month x price of a gallon of gas. Public transportation depends on what the city has to offer.
   - **Food:** The cost of food depends on how much students eat out versus buy at the grocery store. The cost might be $200 to $400 a month.
   - **Medical insurance:** Even if you have good medical insurance through your job, the deductible is usually around $500 to $1,000 a year that must be paid before insurance begins to cover expenses. Without insurance, the typical American spends more than $10,000 a year on medical costs.
   - **Dental insurance:** This may average around $800 a year, depending on if a student has dental insurance and how good it is.
   - **Clothing:** This depends greatly on personal taste. Students may budget to purchase clothes for a very economical price or they can shop at high-end stores that cost a bit more. An average family spends $1,700 a year on clothing, so an individual would be half or a fourth of that.
   - **Health and beauty:** This includes simple things, such as soap, shampoo, toothpaste, tissues, toilet paper, etc.
   - **Household/cleaning supplies:** This is anything students use in their apartments, including what they clean with.
   - **Cell phone:** The cost depends on your plan, but the average cell phone plan is $80 to $200 dollars.

Project 5: Use Technology, Math, and Reasoning

- ▸ **Gifts:** Anytime a holiday, birthday, or anniversary comes along people typically purchase presents. Keep in mind these costs.
- ▸ **Pets:** This depends on the animal you decide to have and the size of it. Having a bird is going to cost a whole lot less than having a large dog. There are food, toys, and vet trips to consider.
- ▸ **Entertainment:** Depending on how much you do, this can be very expensive. Concerts, movies, rentals, and going on vacation all cost money.
- ▸ **Internet:** The averages cost is about $50 to $60 a month.
- ▸ **Donations:** Do you donate to your church, a specific organization, or a specific person? How much you give depends on how much you spend.

Name: _____ Date: _____

Budget Simulation Worksheet

Directions: You have $200 to buy groceries to last you a month. Create a list of groceries you are going to buy and how much of each, keeping a running tally on how much you have spent. When you run out of money, determine if you have enough food to eat for the month or make adjustments to your grocery list.

Item	Unit Price	Number of Item	Total Cost	Notes on Which Meal

Project 5: Use Technology, Math, and Reasoning

Handout 5.1: Budget Simulation Worksheet, *continued*

Item	Unit Price	Number of Item	Total Cost	Notes on Which Meal
Totals				

Name: _____ Date: _____

HANDOUT 5.2

Criteria for Portfolio

Directions: The following criteria are the required elements of your portfolio. You must consider each of them. You may need to do some research in order to determine estimated costs for each element if estimated costs are not provided.

Automatic Deductions

- ▸ -25% of your gross income for taxes and Social Security
- ▸ -5% of your net income for savings and investments

Location: Where you are going to live (city and state) and why you chose this location

Job/Income: Job title, starting monthly salary, benefits

A. **Housing (No Roommates!)**	B. **Transportation:** You must purchase or lease a vehicle, new or used (no more than 3–4 years old), from a dealer. (If you live in a large city that has public transit available, you may choose to deduct $65/month for an unlimited access pass instead of acquiring a vehicle.)
1. Apartment (studio, 1-bedroom, or 2-bedroom)	1. Make, model, and year
2. Rent	2. Purchase price
3. Security deposit	3. Terms of loan (years and interest rate)
4. Utilities (heat, electric, water, garbage pick-up, etc.)	4. Monthly payments
5. Renter's insurance (required)	5. Auto insurance (company and cost)
	6. Deduct $30/month for car repairs
	7. Gas (estimate 1,000 miles a month; calculate your gas consumption based on the MPG for your vehicle)

Handout 5.2: Criteria for Portfolio, *continued*

C. **Essentials:** These items are required. You have to have some money set aside for them, but the actual amount may vary per person.
1. Food (groceries and dining out)
2. Medical insurance cost (research average costs for your state online using a resource such as https://www.valuepenguin.com/average-cost-of-health-insurance#-nogo; estimate costs for physician copays at $15 per visit, and prescriptions at $5 per each prescription refill)
3. Dental insurance cost (insurance covers all cleanings and x-rays; you still need to pay a percentage for fillings, root canals, crowns, orthodontia, etc.)
4. Clothing (a professional occupation needs appropriate clothing; add the cost of a work uniform, if applicable; include shoes/sneakers/coats/swimsuits/underwear, etc.)
5. Health and beauty (just the basics)
6. Household/cleaning supplies
7. Laundry/dry cleaning

D. **Nonessentials (Optional)**
1. Cell phone
2. Gifts (birthdays, Christmas)
3. Haircuts (cuts, coloring, perms, straightening, etc.)
4. Other beauty (tanning, manicures, pedicures, etc.)
5. Pets (food, litter, snacks, toys, vet)
6. Subscriptions (magazines, newspapers, Netflix, etc.)
7. Memberships (health club, AAA, etc.)
8. Entertainment (free time and weekend activities, vacations, movies, video games, etc.)
9. Internet service, cable/satellite
10. Donations (religious, humanitarian, etc.)

Project 5: Use Technology, Math, and Reasoning

HANDOUT 5.3

Researching for Your Portfolio

Directions: You can find almost anything on the Internet, which means you always have to go through a lot of information that might not be relevant to your topic. There are various search engines to help you find information (Yahoo, Google, Bing, etc.).

As you search, you want to be as specific as possible without being too specific. When you are looking for an apartment online, if you search Google using the keyword *apartment,* you retrieve more than 1.4 billion results. How do you refine your search?

Step 1: What Questions Do You Need to Answer?

Determining this will help you determine exactly what information you need. Examples might include:

- What apartments are available?
- What city would this apartment be in?
- In what part of the city do you want your apartment to be?
- How much is the apartment a month?
- How large is the apartment?
- Is there transportation or parking near this apartment?

Step 2: Where Will You Get This Information?

Try to figure out any websites where you might be able to find the answers you are looking for. Examples might include:

- Zillow (https://www.zillow.com)
- Apartments.com (https://www.apartments.com)
- Apartment Finder (https://www.apartmentfinder.com)
- Apartment Guide (https://www.apartmentguide.com)

Step 3: Identify Specific Words

Look over the questions and sources you came up with in Steps 1–2, and circle the important words. This may narrow your search.

Step 4: Search

The Internet is complicated. The trick is to try several combinations of keywords to get you what you specifically want and from whom you want it. Use a safe and reliable search engine, such as Google.

Project 5: Use Technology, Math, and Reasoning

Name: _____ Date: _____

Life Cards

Your car breaks down. You need to pay $180 for a new muffler.	You crack a tooth. You have to pay a $150 deductible.	You decide to adopt a dog. Add $75 in monthly expenses.
You decide to attend a concert. Tickets are $50.	It's your mom's birthday. Spend $30 on a present.	You receive a speeding ticket. Pay $125.
You decide to take a night class. Tuition is $200.	You want to go on a vacation. It costs $250 for your plane ticket.	Your computer breaks down. It costs $100 to repair.
You have won the lottery. You receive $100.	You get a bonus at work. Add $150 to your budget.	It is your birthday. You get a $50 gift card to a restaurant.
You find a lost dog and get a $40 reward.	You get a refund on a TV you bought. Collect $250 dollars.	Your cable bill is free this month due to outages.
You pick up a couple of shifts at work. Increase your monthly salary by $200.	You are walking along the street and stumble across a $20 bill.	You find a $75 check you had forgotten about.

Name: _____ Date: _____

PRODUCT RUBRIC

What If You Paid the Bills?

	Content	Organization	Rationale	Requirements
Excellent	Student covers topic in depth with details and examples. Subject knowledge is excellent.	Content is well organized; headings and bulleted lists are used to group related material.	All decisions are fully explained and justified. Impact of choices has been explicitly addressed.	All requirements are met and exceeded.
Good	Student includes essential knowledge about the topic. Subject knowledge appears to be good, but there are 1–2 factual errors.	Content has some flaws in organization, but headings and bulleted lists are used to organize some information.	Most decisions are explained and justified. Some impact has been considered.	All requirements are met.
Average	Student includes essential information about the topic, but there are 3–4 factual errors.	Content is logically organized for the most part.	Some decisions are justified and explained.	One or two requirements were not completely met.
Needs Improvement	Content is minimal, or there are five or more factual errors.	There was no clear or logical organizational structure, just lots of facts.	Very few, if any, decisions were explained and/or justified.	Three or more requirements were not completely met.

6 Use and Analyze Models

Models bring ideas and concepts to life, making them more practical and easier to understand. We use models a lot in the STEM world. How many students create their own volcano or make a Styrofoam version of the solar system in science class in order to better understand these concepts? Think about architects and structural engineers. When they develop a new building, they do not build the actual structure at first. They construct a model of it so that they can test it and understand what problems need to be addressed before moving on to the actual structure. A perfect example of this would be the Shanghai World Financial Center. In its first designs and model stage, there was a circular opening near the top of the 1,600-foot tall structure to reduce the stresses of wind pressure. However, when architects created the model, they understood the difficulty and expense of making the shape circular. Buildings typically use straight lines in their construction because they are more practical and easier to work with. Because of this, they changed the shape to that of a trapezoid.

Most importantly, models allow us access that we might not have otherwise. We cannot take a student into the center of Earth in order to experience its layers. Not only is this impractical from the standpoint of getting permission slips and liability waivers, but also it is impossible to dig that deep or survive the molten outer core of our planet. However, we can analyze a model of the Earth that shows the different layers, helping students to see something they normally would not be able to see. It would also be challenging to take someone's skull off and poke around in his or her brain in order to understand how it works. But a plastic version of the human brain with removable parts allows someone unlimited access to learn about the brain's structure without risk.

Would students rather read about the rainforest in a book or create a version of the biome complete with producers, consumers, and resources? Would students rather look at photos of the Eiffel Tower or create their own out of toothpicks? Wouldn't it be so much more fun to create a model of New York City that shows the coordinate plane rather than sketching out lines on a worksheet? Models make learning both engaging and authentic. Students learn more through such hands-on activities and actually produce something that others are going to see on display.

Analyzing models also leads to greater understanding. Meteorologists study models of hurricanes in order to try to predict what path one might actually take. Mathematicians spend a lifetime studying models, trying to crack the code that will lead to a new mathematical concept. Engineers study models of new cars and how they react to resistance in wind tunnels to shape the final design of the vehicle. When students create models, they can then analyze other students' models to gain a better understanding. Rather than have each student create a model of the human body, have each student take a different part of the human body and create a more detailed model. If you have 20 students in the classroom, you could have 20 different body parts. When you go to display, set up the classroom like a human body, the brain being at the top, the heart or stomach being in the middle, with the feet being at the bottom. Students can walk around this giant human body, learning about different parts and organs and what they do for the body.

Models are a practical way to study large concepts, and best of all, they bring learning to life. Students are able to interact and study the models so that they see how abstract concepts actually look and function.

Escape Room

In this project, students will create miniature interactive escape room puzzles. Students should construct 2-D or 3-D models of their escape rooms. They must determine the size of their rooms and the materials they will need (e.g., wood, cardboard, LEGOs, Styrofoam, shoe boxes, plastic containers, etc.). Each student's escape room should be themed, and the display should include details that bring the room to life.

Students must include at least 10 math problems for participants to solve. Each math problem should unlock the next problem/clue to escape the room. The math problems must feature at least five different math concepts that work well together, and the problems must increase in difficulty as participants solve each clue. Students' escape rooms should be challenging but not impossible for participants to complete. Escape rooms should be well organized, and participants should be able to move easily from one clue to the next. Students should also include an answer key that clearly shows how each math problem/clue is solved.

At the end of the project, students will display their escape rooms for others to solve as the class hosts an escape room challenge day.

Materials

- ▸ Project Outline: Escape Room (student copies)
- ▸ Suggested Timeline
- ▸ Lesson: What Is an Escape Room?
- ▸ Handout 6.1: Example Escape Room (student copies)
- ▸ Handout 6.2: Escape Room Planning (student copies)
- ▸ Handout 6.3: Peer Review (student copies)
- ▸ Product Rubric: Escape Room (student copies)

PROJECT OUTLINE

Escape Room

Big Idea

Math can be utilized in many contexts.

Essential Question

How can you use math concepts in order to challenge others?

Deliverables

You will create a miniature interactive escape room puzzle. You should construct a 2-D or 3-D model of your escape room. You must determine the size of your room and the materials you will need (e.g., wood, cardboard, LEGOs, Styrofoam, shoe boxes, plastic containers, etc.). Your escape room should be themed, and the display should include details that bring the room to life.

You must include at least 10 math problems for participants to solve. Each math problem should unlock the next problem/clue to escape the room. The math problems must feature at least five different math concepts that work well together, and the problems must increase in difficulty as participants solve each clue. Your escape room should be challenging but not impossible for participants to complete. Your escape room should be well organized, and participants should be able to move easily from one clue to the next. You should also include an answer key that clearly shows how each math problem/clue is solved.

At the end of the project, you will display your escape room for others to solve as the class hosts an escape room challenge day.

Constraints

You must include:
▸ at least 10 different math problems, and
▸ at least five different math concepts in the problems.

SUGGESTED TIMELINE

DAY				
1 Introduce the project and conduct Lesson: What Is an Escape Room? *Ask.*	**2** Have students consider their escape rooms' plans and themes (see Handout 6.2). *Imagine.*	**3** Have students begin planning their escape rooms. *Plan.*	**4** Have students continue planning their escape rooms. *Plan.*	**5** Have students acquire materials to construct their escape rooms. *Plan.*
6 Have students create their escape rooms and 10 problems. *Create.*	**7** Have students create their escape rooms and 10 problems. *Create.*	**8** Have students create their escape rooms and 10 problems. *Create.*	**9** Have students review each other's escape rooms (see Handout 6.3). *Improve.*	**10** Host an escape room challenge day.

Project 6: Use and Analyze Models

LESSON

What Is an Escape Room?

1. Ask students: *Do you know what an escape room is?* Elicit responses. Explain to students that an escape room is a popular interactive puzzle game in which people, as the name suggests, must escape from a room, usually by solving a series of puzzles or clues.

2. Have students experience an escape room for themselves as a class or in groups. Either create an escape room for the class (an excellent resource is https://lock paperscissors.co/wacky-escape-room-themes) or use the one provided. Handout 6.1 includes 10 puzzles and their solutions in order to escape a room. Provide students with the escape room prompt, and then set up the 10 clues around the classroom, each one leading to the next. Clue #1 should be placed under students' seats. Hold on to the answer key and share it with students as needed or at the end of the simulation.

3. (Optional) Using the provided clues on Handout 6.1, set up props around the classroom in order to set the scene for students.

Project 6: Use and Analyze Models

HANDOUT 6.1

Example Escape Room

You have been invited to the mansion of your recently deceased great grandmother, Florence Zelda, for the reading of her will. The reading is held in her study, and you and the other heirs are seated in chairs around the room. Florence Zelda's lawyer begins to read the will. Her will states that the first person to escape the mansion will have the chance to find $1 million. No sooner is this spoken than metal shades drop down over the windows and a loud lock can be heard being activated on the single door in and out of the room. The clues to finding the $1 million are located around the room. You are first instructed to look under the chair you are currently sitting in.

Handout 6.1: Example Escape Room, *continued*

Clue #1

Florence Zelda's desk has nine drawers. They are numbered 1–9. In order to get to the next clue, you must accurately choose which drawer it is in. If you try to open an incorrect drawer, the next clue will be destroyed.

Solve the following two-step equation in order to determine which drawer holds the next clue:

$$2x + 5 = 13$$

Handout 6.1: Example Escape Room, *continued*

Clue #2

Florence Zelda's calendar sits on her desk. Pick the correct date on the calendar by correctly answering the following question:

What is the least common multiple of 12 and 8?

The correct answer will lead you to one of Florence Zelda's favorite things.

Handout 6.1: Example Escape Room, *continued*

Clue #3

It's no secret that Florence Zelda loved Chinese food. Her favorite take-out menu is always on her desk: 24 Chinese Diner. Some of her favorite take-out delicacies are listed below:

Chicken fried rice = $2.50

Wonton soup = $2.15

Egg roll = $2.25

Dumplings = $2.14

Crab sticks = $3.75

Look at the menu and pick the item whose cost is represented by the answer to this problem:

Convert between fractions and decimals: Write 2¼ as a decimal.

The correct answer will lead you to the next clue.

Handout 6.1: Example Escape Room, *continued*

Clue #4

Amongst some other papers on Florence Zelda's desk, you find an old pay stub labeled February 25. It shows she was making $7,200 per hour with her company:

Determine how much she made per second.

Open one of the nine drawers in her desk that corresponds to this answer.

Project 6: Use and Analyze Models

Handout 6.1: Example Escape Room, *continued*

Clue #5

You find a company memo in Florence Zelda's desk. It says that her company hired a new employee every 6 hours, but 3 people were fired every week, and 5 people transferred in a month:

How many employees are added to the company every year?

The answer will unlock the combination lock on Florence Zelda's filing cabinet.

Handout 6.1: Example Escape Room, *continued*

Clue #6

Inside Florence Zelda's filing cabinet, you find instructions for setting the study's thermostat. You must set it correctly in order to get your next clue:

What is the average of all of the following temperatures?

62, 67, 71, 75, 80, 83

Handout 6.1: Example Escape Room, *continued*

Clue #7

Correctly setting the thermostat opens Florence Zelda's drinks cabinet. There is a shelf stocked with large, medium, and small glasses. You must solve the following problem:

3 large glasses contain the same amount of water (in ounces) as 4 medium ones.

3 medium glasses contain the same amount of water (in ounces) as 4 small ones.

How many small glasses would you have to fill in order
to equal the amount in 9 large glasses?

The correct answer will open the storage cabinet next to the drinks cabinet.

Handout 6.1: Example Escape Room, *continued*

Clue #8

The next cabinet opens. Inside is an assortment of office supplies, a magnet, and 10 carabiners. There's a hole in the back of the cabinet: You must put together the carabiners into a circular chain in order to fetch a key that has fallen down the hole. The key unlocks the next cabinet.

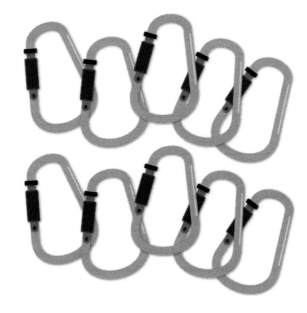

What is the fewest number of chain links that must be opened in order to join the pieces into a circular chain?

Project 6: Use and Analyze Models

Handout 6.1: Example Escape Room, *continued*

Clue #9

The third cabinet contains a map with a variety of random letters marked at various locations, as well as Clue #9 and Clue #10. Using the coordinate plane below, identify which letter on the map represents the location of the buried fortune. Once you have the location, you can solve Clue #10 to escape the room and be the first to find the $1 million.

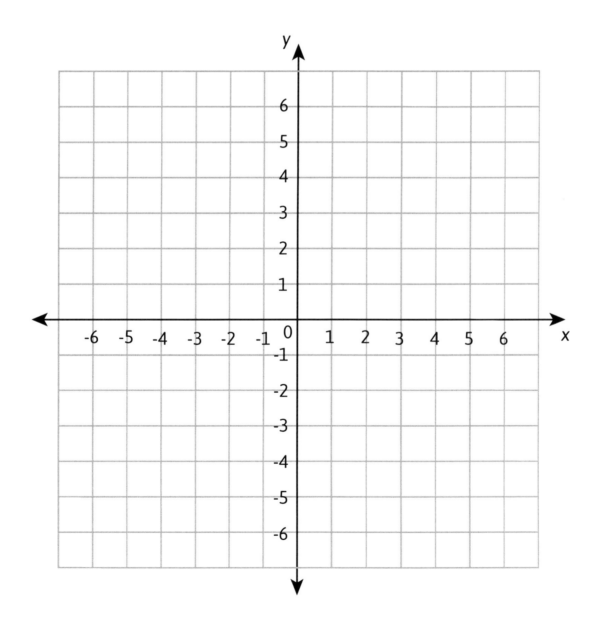

Handout 6.1: Example Escape Room, *continued*

Clue #9, *continued*

Letter #1:
Draw a line from (-3, 1) to (-3, 3) to
   (-2, 3) to (-2, 1)

Draw a line from (-3, 2) to (-2, 2)

Letter #2:
Draw a line from (1, -1) to (1, -3)

Draw a line from (3, -1) to (3, -3)

Draw a line from (1, -2) to (3, -2)

Letter #3:
Draw a line from (-3, -4) to (-5, -4) to
   (-5, -5) to (-3, -5) to (-3, -6) to (-5, -6)

Letter #4:
Draw a line from (2, 3) to (2, 1)

Draw a line from (2, 2) to (4, 3)

Draw a line from (2, 2) to (4, 1)

Letter #5:
Draw a line from (4, -4) to (6, -4)

Draw a line from (5, -4) to (5, -6)

Letter #6:
Draw a line from (-3, -1) to (-1, -1)

Draw a line from (-2, -1) to (-2, -3)

Letter #7:
Draw a line from (7, 3) to (5, 3) to (5, 2) to
   (7, 2) to (7, 1) to (5,1)

Letter #8:
Draw a line from (-2, -6) to (-2, -4) to
   (0, -4) to (0, -5) to (-2, -5)

Letter #9:
Draw a line from (-6, 1) to (-6, 3) to (-5, 3)
   to (-5, 1)

Draw a line from (-5, 3) to (-4, 3) to (-4, 1)

Letter #10:
Draw a line from (-1, 6) to (1, 6) to (-1, 4)
   to (1, 4)

Letter #11:
Draw a line from (1, -6) to (1, -4) to (3, -4)
   to (3, -6) to (1, -6)

Letter #12:
Draw a line from (-1, 1) to (-1, 3) to (1, 3)
   to (1, 2) to (-1, 2) to (1, 1)

Letter #13:
Draw a line from (6, -1) to (4, -1) to (4, -3)
   to (6, -3)

Draw a line from (4, -2) to (6, -2)

Project 6: Use and Analyze Models

Handout 6.1: Example Escape Room, *continued*

Clue #10

The lock on the door to exit the room is a combination lock. Answer the four questions to find the correct sequence.

1. John is 6 years older than Bob and also 4 times older than him. How old is Bob?

2. A dog was given $16, a spider was given $32, and an ant was given $24. Based off of this information, how much money should be given to a robin? (Consider the physical attributes each creature has and how those attributes may have determined how much money it received.)

3. If it is two hours later, then it will take half as much time until it is midnight as it would take if it were an hour later. What time is it?

4. Mr. Jackson has 6 daughters. Each of his daughters has a brother. How many children does Mr. Jackson have?

Handout 6.1: Example Escape Room, *continued*

Answer Key

Clue #1

$2(4) + 5 = 13$
$8 + 5 = 13$
$x = 4$

Clue #2

$2 \times 2 \times 3 = 12$
$2 \times 2 \times 2 = 8$

Repeat each prime factor the most number of times it appears in any of the prime factorizations: 2 appears three times in the factorization of 8, and 3 appears only once in the factorization of 12:

$$2 \times 2 \times 2 \times 3 = 24$$
Day 24

Clue #3

2.25 = Egg roll

Clue #4

$60 \times 60 = 3{,}600$ seconds in an hour
$\$7{,}200 \div 3{,}600$ seconds = $\$2$
$\$2$ per second

Clue #5

24 hours in a day $\div$ 6 hours = 4 employees hired every day $\times$ 365 days = 1,460 added
52 weeks in a year $\times$ 3 people fired a week = 156 subtracted
12 months in a year $\times$ 5 transfers a month = 60 added
$1{,}460 - 156 + 60 = 1{,}364$ employees added every year

Handout 6.1: Example Escape Room, *continued*

Clue #6

$62 + 67 + 71 + 75 + 80 + 83 = 438$
$438 \div 6 = 73$
73 degrees

Clue #7

3 large = 4 medium = common denominator of 12
Large = 3×4 ounces = 12
Medium = 4×3 ounces = 12
Large = 4 ounces
Medium = 3 ounces

3 medium = 4 small
Medium = 3 ounces
9 ounces total
9 ounces $\div$ 4 small = 2.25 ounces small
9 large glasses $\times$ 4 ounces per glass = 36 total ounces
36 ounces $\div$ 2.25 ounces per small = 16 small glasses
16

Clue #8

5 open carabiners would be enough to join them into a circular chain. You open up a carabiner and link it to two other carabiners that don't need to be opened. Repeat until you have all 10 linked together.

Clue #9

Z marks the spot.

Handout 6.1: Example Escape Room, *continued*

Clue #10

1. 2
2. Dog = 4 legs; $16 \div 4 = 4$
   Spider = 8 legs; $32 \div 8 = 4$
   Ant = 6 legs; $24 \div 4 = 4$
   Robin = 2 legs; $2 \times 4 = 8$
   Answer: \$8 (\$4 per leg)

3. 9
4. 7

The combination is 2897.

Project 6: Use and Analyze Models

HANDOUT 6.2

Escape Room Planning

Directions: Before you begin to create your escape room, you should plan out what your escape room is going to look like, from its theme to its setup to the positioning of the clues.

Selecting a Theme

Your escape room needs to have a strong theme. As an example, your location may determine your theme. Perhaps your escape room is set on a train, in a haunted mansion, in the midst of a museum heist, or at a baseball field.

Determining the Size of Your Escape Room

The escape room centers around your theme. You need to include props, set dressing, characters, situations, and rooms that have to do with the theme. If your escape room is set at a baseball field, you might have a few smaller rooms within your escape room, such as a dugout, the field, a locker room, or a concession stand. These rooms might dictate the size of your escape room and how many materials you need to collect in order to construct it.

Developing Your Scenario and Your Clues

The theme and size of your escape room will determine where you locate puzzles. If there's more than one room, each room could have a couple of puzzles. Your escape room clues must involve math. You must have at least 10 problems for participants to solve and utilize five different math concepts (in other words, you should not have 10 multiplication problems or 10 division problems).

Hints on Planning Your Escape Room

- ▸ Draw neatly or design your escape room on a computer.
- ▸ Use proper drawing tools (e.g., ruler, compass).
- ▸ Label the different parts of the design, writing clearly in print.
- ▸ Make sure your theme is consistent throughout the escape room.

Handout 6.2: Escape Room Planning, *continued*

▸ Be sure there are at least 10 problems, with at least five different math concepts used.
▸ Ensure that the problems get more challenging throughout.

Sample Escape Room Plan

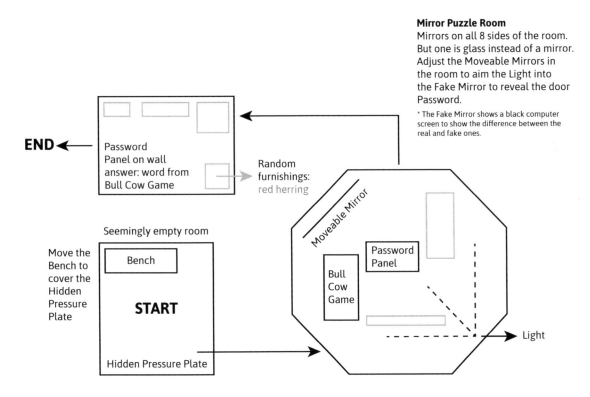

Mirror Puzzle Room
Mirrors on all 8 sides of the room. But one is glass instead of a mirror. Adjust the Moveable Mirrors in the room to aim the Light into the Fake Mirror to reveal the door Password.

* The Fake Mirror shows a black computer screen to show the difference between the real and fake ones.

Project 6: Use and Analyze Models

Name: _____ Date: _____

Peer Review

Directions: Review a classmate's escape room. Answer the following questions.

1. Does your classmate's escape room meet the requirements of 10 math problems?

2. Are there five different math concepts utilized amongst the 10 problems?

3. Is the math used in the problems correct?

4. Is an answer key provided?

5. Is the escape room challenging but not impossible?

Handout 6.3: Peer Review, *continued*

6. Does the escape room have a theme?

7. How is the theme displayed?

8. Does the model look professional?

9. Are there any details you feel this escape room is missing?

PRODUCT RUBRIC

Escape Room

	Organization	Math	Display
Excellent	Escape room includes more than 10 problems for participants to solve. More than five different math concepts are included. An answer key is provided and is easy to understand.	All math involved in the escape room is correct. The different math concepts included work together, and clues increase in difficulty from the first to the last. Answer key shows how each problem is solved step by step.	Escape room has a clear, inventive theme that is followed through-out. Display looks like a miniature version of the room; details and accents bring it to life. Display is easy for participants to use; it is easy to move from one clue to the next.
Good	Escape room includes at least 10 problems for participants to solve. Five different math concepts are included. An answer key is provided, but it is not always easy to understand.	Most of the math is correct; there are one or two mistakes. The different math concepts work well together, but the clues do not always increase in difficulty from the first to the last. Answer key is mostly correct, but it does not always show how problems are solved step by step.	Escape room has a theme that is followed throughout all of the problems and rooms, but it could be more creative. Display looks like a miniature version of the room; some details and accents bring it to life. Display is easy for participants to use for the most part; some areas cause confusion.
Needs Improvement	Escape room includes fewer than 10 problems for participants to solve. Fewer than five math concepts are included. An answer key either is not provided or is very difficult to follow.	There are many math mistakes. The different math concepts do not always work together logically. Answer key has many mistakes or does not show how the problems are solved.	Escape room does not have a theme that is followed throughout. Display is very basic; it lacks details and accents that could bring it to life. Display is not always easy for participants to use, making it difficult to get through the clues.

Project 6: Use and Analyze Models

7 Record and Analyze Data

One of the most important things STEM professionals must do while conducting an experiment or research is to record the data they collect. This is because they are following the engineering design process, and if they wish to replicate their results, they need to keep track of what they did.

Recording data over time can be a valuable tool. We do this with students, recording grades and evaluations over the course of the year to determine whether the student is ready to move on to the next level. We use this data to adjust our teaching and ensure that students get what they need in the classroom, so we are constantly analyzing the data to inform our decisions. We record data in the form of memories and use it to make decisions all of the time. For example, if a person goes to a restaurant and receives bad service, he or she is probably going to be hesitant to return. If the person does go back and feels treated badly a second time, it is very unlikely this person will ever eat at this restaurant again. Businesses analyze data to predict what they need to do in order to turn a profit. They look at the history of sales and how the market is trending. They then try to predict whether the trends will continue, or they can make changes to try to increase profits.

The key is to organize data so that it can be understood and interpreted. Students need to be shown what organizational tools are at their disposal and then decide which ones will best display their data. The best graphic organizer to use is the one that will allow anyone to access and understand the data. That means properly labeling and having a key so that others can understand what the data are showing.

Organizing data is a good skill for students, especially gifted ones, to learn and practice. Students sometimes have grandiose notions but cannot funnel them into a form that can be shared and reflected on with others. Learning how to do this will lead to more purposeful reflection. Through reflection, the most valuable learning takes place. There is sometimes a difference between what you want students to learn and what they actually learn. And each student might have a different takeaway from a lesson or activity. It is important to create space where students can reflect upon their own learning. Sometimes students do this through portfolios in which they build a collect of their own work over the course of a semester or year. To make a portfolio meaningful, students need to analyze how or if they have grown over the course of the year. This is where that reflection takes place. Whenever students are looking at data over time, there needs to be an opportunity for them to reflect upon what was learned.

Math Portfolio

In this project, students will create a portfolio that represents their math learning over a 3-month period. They must include at least five examples of what they learned and reflect on each of the five works. They must also include their favorite mistake and what they learned from it. Students' reflections should show an understanding of what they learned at a deep level, identify their strengths and weakness and ways to improve them, and present a clear plan of how to use what they learned in future work. Students' portfolios should be well organized and include a table of contents and/or tabs so that they are easy to navigate. At the end of the project, students will defend what they learned to a panel. Your panel can be made up of older students, teachers, parents, or any people from occupations that use math (e.g., accounting, pharmacy).

Materials

- ► Student computer and Internet access
- ► Project Outline: Math Portfolio (student copies)
- ► Suggested Timeline
- ► Lesson: What Is Reflection?
- ► Handout 7.1: Representing Your Learning (student copies)
- ► Handout 7.2: Your Favorite Mistake (student copies)
- ► Handout 7.3: Defending Your Portfolio (student copies)
- ► Product Rubric: Math Portfolio (student copies)

PROJECT OUTLINE

Math Portfolio

Big Idea

Making a mistake can be when the most learning occurs.

Essential Question

What have you learned?

Deliverables

You will create a portfolio that represents your math learning over a 3-month period. You must include at least five examples of what you learned and reflect on each of the five works. You must also include your favorite mistake and what you learned from it. Your reflections should show an understanding of what you learned at a deep level, identify your strengths and weakness and ways to improve them, and present a clear plan of how to use what you learned in future work. Your portfolio should be well organized and include a table of contents and/or tabs so that it is easy to navigate. At the end of the project, you will defend what you learned to a panel.

Constraints

You must:
- include math work from the last 3 months,
- include at least five different examples of work with reflections, and
- orally defend your portfolio.

SUGGESTED TIMELINE

DAY				
1 Introduce the project and conduct Lesson: What Is Reflection? *Ask.*	**2** Have students choose works that represent their learning (see Handout 7.1). *Imagine.*	**3** Have students determine their favorite mistakes (see Handout 7.2). *Plan.*	**4** Have students reflect on their first work. *Create.*	**5** Have students reflect on their second work. *Create.*
6 Have students reflect on their third work. *Create.*	**7** Have students reflect on their fourth work. *Create.*	**8** Have students reflect on their fifth work. *Create.*	**9** Have students prepare their defenses (see Handout 7.3). *Improve.*	**10** Have students present their defenses.

LESSON

What Is Reflection?

1. Explain to students that what you, as the teacher, think students learn and what they actually learn might be two very different things. Students might experience the same thing: They may not realize what they have learned after a lesson is over. Reflecting on what they learned can help them find out the true picture.

2. Usually the best way to reflect is to ask effective questions that cause one to think a little more about the process. Here are some examples of prompts you can use with students to spark their thinking:

    ▸ What was your favorite lesson? Why did you like it so much?

    ▸ During which lesson did you struggle? Were you able to overcome this struggle, or did you simply get stuck?

    ▸ What method of teaching has been the most effective manner for you to learn math? Why was it so effective?

    ▸ How important do you think it is to practice the math concepts you are learning?

    ▸ What method of teaching has been the least effective manner for you to learn math? Why?

    ▸ What math concept did you learn that you have had to use in several different lessons?

    ▸ What math concept do you think is going to be useful later on in life?

    ▸ If you had to teach one math concept to the class, what would it be and why would you choose it?

    ▸ What did you learn from your classmates? Was this a good thing or bad thing?

    ▸ When you think back to all of your schooling, which lesson on math stands out the most, good or bad, and why?

3. As students reflect on what they learned, they might also consider a model to follow, such as What?/So What?/Now What?:

    ▸ What? (Descriptive)

        ▹ Describe what happened without using any judgment.

        ▹ Include facts, what happened, with whom, etc.

        ▹ What was the result of the work?

- So what? (Shift from descriptive to interpretive)
  - ▷ What is the meaning of the experience for each participant?
  - ▷ What are the feelings involved and the lessons learned?
  - ▷ Take the "what" from the descriptive stage and explain the "why."

- Now what? (Plan for moving forward)
  - ▷ Contextual: Describe this situation's place in the big picture.
  - ▷ Apply lessons learned/insights gained to new situations.
  - ▷ Set future goals, creating an action plan.

Project 7: Record and Analyze Data

Name: _____ Date: _____

Representing Your Learning

Directions: After you have collected work from the past 3 months that you feel represents what you have learned, you need to select just five examples of work. Some criteria for selecting works that represent your learning include:

- The example of work is complete and substantial.
- The work was challenging.
- The work shows growth.
- You are including a variety of types of work (i.e., not just five tests or five homework assignments).
- You might include more than written work. If the work was more performance-based, write up what you did and how you did it. If the work was completed in a group, have one of your members write about your contributions.

Do not . . .

- pick something just because you got a good grade,
- pick something that was easy for you,
- include several works that demonstrate the same skill,
- avoid using something because you made a lot of mistakes, or
- be afraid to share something that you learned that you do not think the teacher wants to hear. This is about your learning.

HANDOUT 7.2

Your Favorite Mistake

Directions: Making a mistake is often when the most learning takes place. Embrace mistakes and and figure out the lessons you learned. Fail actually means **F**irst **A**ttempt **I**n **L**earning.

Consider your work over the past 3 months and try to find the biggest mistake you made. This does not need to be an entire lesson or test or homework. It can be a single problem or something you did not do but should have.

1. What was the original work?

2. What mistake did you make?

3. Correct the work.

4. Why was this your favorite mistake?

5. What did you learn from the mistake?

6. Would you make this mistake again? Why or why not?

Project 7: Record and Analyze Data

Name: _____ Date: _____

Defending Your Portfolio

Directions: You must defend your portfolio. You are not going to present all five examples of your work, but they will all be read by the evaluator. For your defense, you should choose the one you feel best exhibits what you learned and shows your growth and progress.

Essential Question: What is the most important lesson I learned in the past 3 months in math?

In your defense, you need to:

▸ Be clear about what the original lesson was.
▸ Include examples to prove what you learned.
▸ Show how you achieved mastery of the lesson.
▸ Explain the rationale for why you feel it is such an important lesson.
▸ Be able to answer any follow-up questions the panel/teacher might have with meaningful responses that show you have reflected on the work.
▸ Share your favorite mistake and what you learned from making that mistake.

You must defend your portfolio in a professional manner:
▸ Make occasional eye contact.
▸ Stand up straight.
▸ Do not put your hands in your pockets or cross your arms.
▸ Speak clearly and loudly enough to be heard.

Name: _____ Date: _____

PRODUCT RUBRIC

Math Portfolio

	Defense of Portfolio	Portfolio	Reflections
Excellent	Student presents in a professional manner, speaking clearly and confidently throughout. Student makes a clear case for the growth that has been made over the course of 3 months, using lots of evidence to make the point from the example. Student is able to answer any questions that are asked with meaningful answers that show reflection of work.	Portfolio features five or more examples of work that clearly show the students' progress over 3 months. Portfolio is well organized; a table of contents and/or tabs are included.	Reflections show an understanding of what was learned at a deeper level. Student identifies strengths and weaknesses and ways to improve these. Student has a clear plan on how to use what was learned in future work.
Good	Student presents in a professional manner, speaking clearly and confidently, but not consistently throughout. Student makes a case for the progress that has been made over the course of 3 months, but could use more evidence to make the point. Student is able to answer most questions but does not always include meaningful answers that show reflection of work.	Portfolio features three or four examples of work that show the students' progress over 3 months. Portfolio is organized with a table of contents and/or tabs, but it is not always easy to navigate.	Reflections show an understanding of what was learned but is not introspective, just content. Student identifies strengths and weaknesses but not how to improve them. Student has ideas of how to use what was learned in future work but no clear plan.

Name: _____ Date: _____

Product Rubric: Math Portfolio, *continued*

	Defense of Portfolio	Portfolio	Reflections
Needs Improvement	Student does not present in a professional manner; student does not speak clearly or confidently. Student does not make a case for the progress that has been made over the course of 3 months. Student is not able to answer most questions, or answers do not show an understanding of learning.	Portfolio features two or fewer examples of work that show the students' progress over 3 months. Portfolio is not organized; it lacks a table of contents and/or tabs, making it difficult to navigate.	Reflections do not show an understanding of what was learned. Student does not identify strengths and/or weaknesses. Student does not have a plan for using what was learned in future work.

Project 7: Record and Analyze Data

8 Investigate Change Over Time and Patterns

One of the most valuable things you can teach students is that history repeats itself. Consider World War I and World War II, the assassinations of Abraham Lincoln and John F. Kennedy, and the fall of the Greek and Roman Empires. Students may wonder, "How do you avoid history repeating itself?" The answer is: by learning from it. By studying patterns and trends, students can make educated predictions. Consider global warming and climate change. Scientists have noticed a trend that the world is getting warmer, as pollution destroys the ozone a little bit every year. As a result of this pattern, humans are working to combat climate change by cutting down on emissions that cause this deterioration.

Patterns are evident in the advancement of technology, with a new iPhone coming out each year, computers getting smaller and smarter, and self-driving cars becoming more commonplace. It is the study of these advances in technology that leads to further advancements. We are constantly trying to make things better. It is human nature. By studying changes over time, we are able to determine what we do not need anymore, what we need to continue to do, and what we need to add to improve something.

In the classroom, we do not have the luxury of studying something firsthand over a long period of time. But we can run an experiment for a few weeks, chart observations over a limited period of time, run a brief investigation of what may happen, and study the past to determine how elements change over time.

We Didn't Start the Fire

In this project, students will work in groups to create a multi-tiered timeline using the Billy Joel song "We Didn't Start the Fire." Students will need to determine the events discussed in the song, research the significance of the events and terms in the song, and divide the events into three categories—the United States, the United States in foreign lands, and international. Each category mentioned will be on one tier of the timeline. Students must make at least five connections between events from different tiers. How students choose to display their timelines is up to them, but the relationships between tiers must be clear. Students must ensure their timelines' tiers are in chronological order and that all group members contribute equally to the project.

Note. The song "We Didn't Start the Fire" stops in the 1980s because it was written in 1989. As a bonus activity, groups can write stanzas for the 1990s and 2000s. Students will have to include important events from these decades and write at least eight lines for each decade.

Materials

- ▸ Project Outline: We Didn't Start the Fire (student copies)
- ▸ Suggested Timeline
- ▸ Lesson: What Is Cause and Effect?
- ▸ Lesson: Developing Timelines
- ▸ Product Rubric: We Didn't Start the Fire (student copies)

PROJECT OUTLINE

We Didn't Start the Fire

Big Idea

Events in one country can effect events across the world.

Essential Question

How does cause and effect influence major events in history?

Deliverables

You will work in a group to create a multi-tiered timeline using the Billy Joel song "We Didn't Start the Fire." You will need to:

1. determine the events discussed in the song,
2. research the significance of the events and terms in the song, and
3. divide the events into three categories—the United States, the United States in foreign lands, and international.

Each category will be one tier of the timeline. You must make at least five connections between events from different tiers. How you choose to display your timeline is up to you, but the relationships between tiers must be clear. You must ensure your timeline's tiers are in chronological order and that all group members contribute equally to the project.

Constraints

You must:

▶ use the Billy Joel song "We Didn't Start the Fire,"
▶ include three tiers in your timeline, and
▶ make five logical connections between events in different tiers of your timeline.

Bonus Activity

The song "We Didn't Start the Fire" stops in the 1980s because it was written in 1989. As a bonus activity, your group can write stanzas for the 1990s and 2000s. You will have to include important events from these decades and write at least eight lines for each decade.

Project 8: Investigate Change Over Time and Patterns

SUGGESTED TIMELINE

DAY				
1 Introduce the project and conduct Lesson: What Is Cause and Effect? *Ask/ Imagine.*	**2** Conduct Lesson: Developing Timelines and divide students into groups. *Ask.*	**3** Have groups research events from the song. *Plan.*	**4** Have groups research events from the song. *Plan.*	**5** Have groups research events from the song. *Plan.*
6 Have groups construct their timelines. *Create.*	**7** Have groups construct their timelines. *Create.*	**8** Have groups make cause-and-effect connections. *Create.*	**9** Have groups make cause-and-effect connections. *Create.*	**10** Have groups check their timelines and turn them in. *Improve.*

LESSON

What Is Cause and Effect?

1. Explain to students that the chronology of events can sometimes be more important than knowing the exact date an event occurred. Chronology shows how one event may have led to another. Chronology can show cause and effect. Share with students an example (e.g., humans invented the wheel, then wagons, then cars, and without the wheel, other innovations may not have occurred).

2. Ask: Can you think of some other causes and effects in history? Sample responses may include:
   ▸ The discovery of fire allowed humans to cook food and enabled them to live longer.
   ▸ Archduke Franz Ferdinand of Austria was assassinated in 1914, which lead to World War I and the United States eventually entering the war.
   ▸ The invention of computers led to the Internet and eventually Wi-Fi.

3. Explain that one way to examine cause and effect is by developing timelines of events, which students will learn more about in the next lesson. Ask students to consider how cause and effect influences their own lives. Ask: *What are some activities you do each morning, afternoon, or evening?* Students might consider how they wake up, eat breakfast, brush their teeth, and then go to school, or they might consider how they take the bus home from school, do their homework, eat dinner, etc.

4. Ask: *How do some of these events lead to others?* Guide students to understand that certain events must precede others (e.g., going to school means you may have homework, taking the bus home from school means you can eat dinner at home, getting ready for bed allows you to go to sleep, etc.).

5. Play the song "We Didn't Start the Fire" by Billy Joel (available on YouTube at https://www.youtube.com/watch?v=eFTLKWw542g) for the class. Explain that there are many events and terms mentioned in the song, many of which are effects of preceding events. As students begin to work on this project, they will need to analyze the lyrics (available online from several sources, such as https://www.azlyrics.com/lyrics/billyjoel/wedidntstartthefire.html) before they develop their timelines.

Project 8: Investigate Change Over Time and Patterns

LESSON

Developing Timelines

1. Explain that history is divided up into two major eras: BC (Before Christ) or BCE (Before Common Era) and AD (Anno Domini—in the year of our Lord) or CE (Common Era).

2. Have students develop timelines of 5–10 events in their own lives. Students can include major events before they were born (e.g., their parents' births) and label the timeline BM (Before Me) and AM (After Me). The Year 0 is when they are born. See Figure 5 for an example. Ask students to consider events that have had or will have long-term effects on their lives. Afterward, discuss students' work.

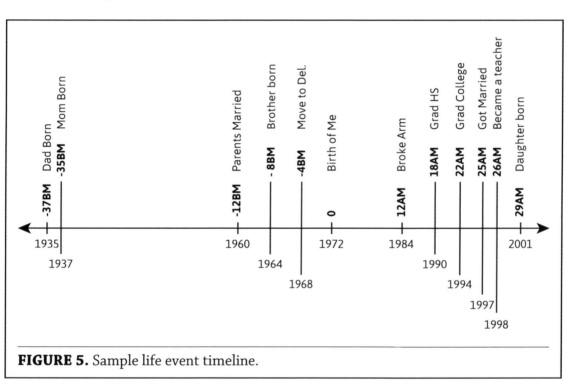

FIGURE 5. Sample life event timeline.

3. Explain that, for this project, students' timelines will be more complicated than the timelines they just created. Multi-tiered timelines have multiple tiers so that it is easy to compare and contrast events and identify causes and effects. See Figure 6 for an example.

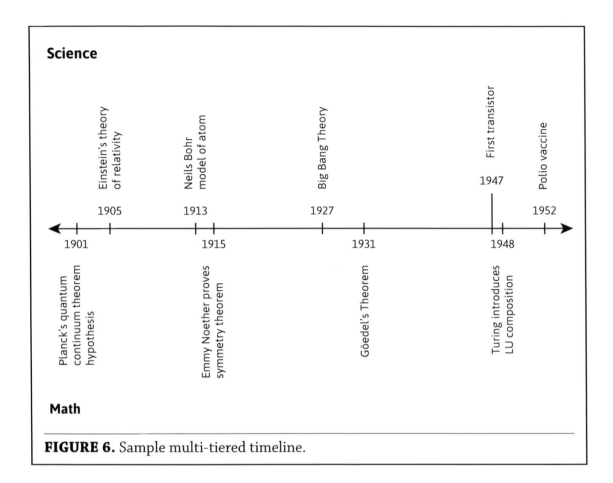

FIGURE 6. Sample multi-tiered timeline.

4. Explain that events, especially major discoveries or new innovations, do not happen in a vacuum. Once they are introduced, these ideas go into the world and influence others. For example, Albert Einstein's theory of relativity likely had a large influence on the math and science community in general.

5. Play the song "We Didn't Start the Fire" by Billy Joel for students again as needed. Remind them that they will need to carefully research the events in order to develop the tiers of their timelines and recognize connections between the events.

Project 8: Investigate Change Over Time and Patterns

PRODUCT RUBRIC

We Didn't Start the Fire

	Timelines	Connections	Group Work
Excellent	Timelines are in chronological order and easy to follow. The three timelines line up with one another so that the years are consistent. The three timelines are well organized and presented in a professional manner.	Logical connections are made between many events from different timelines. The significance of the connections is explained clearly and in detail. At least 10 connections are made.	Group used class time wisely, always on task and getting goals accomplished. Project was turned in on time. Group members divided the tasks equally.
Good	Timelines are in chronological order but are not always organized. The three timelines line up with one another for the most part, but a few years are out of place. The three timelines are well organized but not always presented in a professional manner.	Logical connections are made between events from different timelines, but some connections are overlooked. The significance of the connections is explained but not in detail. Six to nine connections are made.	Group used class time wisely for the most part, but group members were not always on task. Project was a little late, and/or some minor details were not completed until the last minute. Group members divided the tasks, but some group members had to do more work than others.
Needs Improvement	Timelines are not in chronological order. The three timelines do not line up with one another. The three timelines are not well organized; they are hard to follow.	Few logical connections are made between events from different timelines. The significance of the connections is not explained or lacks any detail. Fewer than six connections are made.	Group did not always use class time wisely, frequently off task. Project was very late, and/or entire sections were not completed. One or two group members did all the work for everyone else.

9 Use Computer Models or Simulations

As technology becomes more and more prevalent in education, so, too, does the issue of using it properly. Technology, like any tool, is only effective if it improves learning. There are several ways to use technology to enhance the learning of students, but one that is especially effective is the use of computer models, which allow students to ask "What if . . . ?" What if this happened instead of that, what if this had never happened, or what if we did it differently? Computer models allow students to try their solution in different ways. They can make three or four attempts at something, changing something major or just making minor tweaks, leading them closer and closer to a functional solution. Computer models allow students to fail with a safety net in place. If a student were making a model out of craft sticks only to find out halfway through that he made a mistake in his foundation, he would have to throw the entire thing out and start with new materials.

The computer program *Sim City* is an excellent example. You can build entire cities, including infrastructure, buildings, and other items crucial to the success of a city. The program alerts you if your city is not performing like it should. If you do not string enough electricity throughout the city, there are homes and businesses that will be without electricity. This makes it difficult for them to be successful. If you put the fire department on one side of town only to have a fire break out on the complete opposite side, by the time the fire truck gets to its destination, the building will have burned down. If the town becomes too unhappy, you start to lose residents, and when that happens, you lose money needed to keep building. If you have enough problems with the city, you can simply hit the destruct button and bring the whole thing to the ground and start all over again.

How many times were you playing a video game, such as *Donkey Kong*, only to either be hit by a barrel, caught on fire by a fireball, or have the bouncy thing land on your head? When failure happened, what did you do? You put another quarter in the slot and tried again. You would try and fail for hours on end. Nowadays with Microsoft Xbox, Nintendo Switch, and Sony PlayStation, simply pushing a button allows you to try again. This process is all about learning—learning what you did wrong, learning what not to do, learning what works. This is the sort of resilience we should bring into the classroom.

Computer simulations make problem solving more authentic because they put students in the shoes of the person or people experiencing the problem, and they are also excellent examples of learning from failure. Using computer simulations and models to teach students that failure is okay encourages students to take risks. Taking a risk is where the most learning takes place. This is the power technology can have in the classroom.

Planning a Road Trip

In this project, students will work in groups to plan a simulation for a one-way road trip involving at least three people to somewhere in the United States. They will plot which roads they need to take to reach their final destinations, how many miles they will travel, where they will stay along the way, and other details. They will also submit a budget for how much they will spend on the trip, including for meals and sightseeing.

Students can select destinations where they have never been, attractions they have always wanted to see, places where family lives, places where they have been before but enjoy, etc. Students must start their trips from where they currently live. They have 7 days for the vacation, including their travel time, so they must plan their road trip carefully. At the end of the project, students will share their trips with the class in a gallery walk.

Materials

- ▸ Project Outline: Planning a Road Trip (student copies)
- ▸ Suggested Timeline
- ▸ Lesson: Planning a Class Trip
- ▸ Handout 9.1: Choosing Your Destination (student copies)
- ▸ Product Rubric: Planning a Road Trip (student copies)

PROJECT OUTLINE

Planning a Road Trip

Big Idea

Planning is key to a successful trip.

Essential Question

If you could go anywhere in the United States, where would you go, and how would you plan your trip?

Deliverables

You will work in a group to plan a road trip for at least three people to somewhere in the United States. You will plot which roads you need to take to reach your final destinations, how many miles you will travel, where you will stay along the way, and other details. You will also submit a budget for how much you will spend on the trip, including for meals and sightseeing.

You can select a destination where you have never been, an attraction you have always wanted to see, a place where family lives, a place where you have been before but enjoy, etc. You must start your trips from where you currently live. You have 7 days for the vacation, including your travel time, so you must plan your road trip carefully:

1. Where will you travel?
2. How many miles will you travel?
3. How long will it take you to travel this distance by car?
4. Where will you visit along the way?
5. Where will you eat along the way?
6. Where will you stay along the way?

At the end of the project, you will share your simulated trip with the class in a gallery walk.

Project Outline: Planning a Road Trip, *continued*

Constraints

You must:

- ▸ travel to a location in the United States,
- ▸ travel by car,
- ▸ create a budget for how much the trip will cost
- ▸ use an online program to plot your trip,
- ▸ only use 7 days for the entire one-way trip.

SUGGESTED TIMELINE

DAY				
1 Introduce the project and divide students into groups. *Ask.*	**2** Conduct Lesson: Planning a Class Trip. *Imagine.*	**3** Have groups research possible destinations. *Imagine.*	**4** Have groups choose their destinations. *Imagine.*	**5** Have groups research the distance they must travel. *Plan.*
6 Have groups determine the distance they must travel. *Plan.*	**7** Have groups decide where they are going to stay on their trips. *Plan.*	**8** Have groups determine the cost of where they are going to stay. *Plan.*	**9** Have groups decide where they are going to eat during their trips. *Plan.*	**10** Have groups decide on a budget for what they are going to eat during their trips. *Plan.*
11 Have groups decide what attractions they are going to see on their trips. *Plan.*	**12** Have groups estimate the cost of the attractions they are going to see on their trips. *Plan.*	**13** Have groups determine the entire budget for the trip. *Plan.*	**14** Have groups double-check the budget for their trips. *Improve.*	**15** Have groups begin to create their maps. *Create.*
16 Have groups continue to create their maps. *Create.*	**17** Have groups continue to create their maps. *Create.*	**18** Have groups continue to create their maps. *Create.*	**19** Have groups check that their maps and budgets correlate. *Improve.*	**20** Host a gallery walk where groups display their trips.

Planning a Class Trip

1. Tell students that as a class, you are going to plan a trip to Disney World in Orlando, FL. Your starting destination is Chicago, IL.
2. Ask: *How many miles do you think it is from Chicago to Orlando?* Use an online map service (Google Maps, MapQuest, etc.) to find the distance. The trip is about 1,161 miles by car.
3. The map shows that the trip will take about 17 hours and 19 minutes—almost an entire day. Explain that you will need to stop for gas, get something to eat, take bathroom breaks, stretch your legs, etc. You might even want to break the trip into a couple of days if you want to stop anywhere else on the way, such as Nashville, TN. Nashville is about halfway into the trip—it's 470 miles away, or 7.5 hours. Tell the class you will spend the night in Nashville and head to Orlando the following day to complete the remaining 685 miles.
4. Say: Next, we need to decide on places we would like to visit. Our two main stops are Nashville and Orlando. Nashville is just a single day, possibly two if we stop there on the way back. In Orlando, we will be staying for 5 days, so we need to plan for that.
5. Explain: The attractions we plan to visit will determine whether the budget will be high or low. For instance, if we go to a place that has an admission charge, that is going to increase our budget. However, if we go to a free venue, such as a park or a shopping plaza, the budget will be lower.
6. Share with students some attractions in Nashville, such as:
   ▸ The Country Music Hall of Fame (general admission is about $25)
   ▸ Nashville Shores Water Park ($32)
   ▸ Grand Ole Opry ($40–$100)
   ▸ Edwin and Percy Warner Parks (free)

7. Have students decide where they think the class should go.
8. Explain that the class also needs to choose some activities to do in Orlando, such as:
   ▸ Walt Disney World (about $100 a day)
   ▸ Universal Studios Florida (about $170 a day)
   ▸ Universal CityWalk (free)
   ▸ SeaWorld Orlando ($100)
   ▸ Lake Eola Park (free)
   ▸ Medieval Times Dinner & Tournament ($63)

9. As the class chooses its destinations, keep a running tally of the cost of all of them.

10. Tell students: When it comes to eating, you do not need to pick a specific restaurant unless you are going someplace specific, like one of the many themed restaurants at Universal Studios and Disney World. You can indicate what type of venue you are going to.
    ▸ Fast food (e.g., McDonalds, Burger King, Taco Bell): $6 a person
    ▸ Sit-down restaurant, lower budget (e.g., Cracker Barrel, Big Boy, Steak and Shake): $10 a person
    ▸ Sit-down family restaurant, higher budget (e.g., Applebees, Olive Garden): $15 a person
    ▸ Pizza: $20 per pizza
    ▸ Higher end restaurant: $20+ a person

11. Explain: You can always plan to buy groceries and make some meals, but you will need to estimate how much you will spend on groceries.

12. Explain that the class will have to determine how many meals it is going to eat on the trip. For the trip to Orlando, the class has to plan for 7 days of food (2 travel days, 5 at the destination), or 21 meals.

13. Go through each day of the trip and have the class pick meal options for every meal. Keep a running tally.

14. The final question the class needs to answer is where the class will sleep during the trip for 6 nights:
    ▸ Campgrounds: $30 a night
    ▸ Motel: $50 a night
    ▸ Lower budget hotel: $75 a night
    ▸ Mid-budget hotel: $100 a night
    ▸ Higher budget hotel: $150 a night

15. Have the class decide where to stay throughout the trip, and keep a running tally of how much it is going to cost.

16. As a class, calculate the final budget (destinations + food + accommodations).

Name: _____ Date: _____

Choosing Your Destination

Directions: Select potential destinations for your road trip. Remember, your destination can be somewhere you have never been, an attraction you have always wanted to see, a place where family lives, a place where you have been before but enjoy, etc. You may do some research on destinations if you wish.

Choice #1: _____

The reason I am choosing it: _____

_____

_____

How many days of travel it might take: _____

Choice #2: _____

The reason I am choosing it: _____

_____

_____

How many days of travel it might take: _____

Choice #3: _____

The reason I am choosing it: _____

_____

_____

How many days of travel it might take: _____

Project 9: Use Computer Models or Simulations

PRODUCT RUBRIC

Planning a Road Trip

	Itinerary	Budget	Map
Excellent	Each day is clearly scheduled and described in detail from beginning to end. Itinerary includes alternatives, should there be inclement weather or scheduling issues.	Budget carefully details how much money will be spent on attractions, lodging, and food.	Map looks professional, with everything in proper proportion. Map is properly labeled; it is clear how many miles the route is, what roads will be taken, and which destinations are along the way. Map is large enough for viewers to see during the gallery walk.
Good	Each day is scheduled, but the itinerary is not very detailed. Itinerary includes a couple of alternatives, should there be inclement weather or scheduling issues.	Budget includes how much money will be spent on attractions, lodging, and food, but more detail could be provided.	Map looks somewhat professional, with everything in proper proportion, but some areas are sloppy. Map is mostly labeled; for the most part, it is clear how many miles the route is, what roads will be taken, or which destinations are a long the way, but it could be more detailed. Map is of good size, but it could be larger to enable viewers to see during the gallery walk.
Needs Improvement	Days are not well scheduled and no details are provided. Itinerary does not include any alternatives.	Budget does not include how much money will be spent on attractions, lodging, and food.	Map does not look professional; many parts are out of proportion. Map is not properly labeled. Map is not large enough for viewers to see well during the gallery walk.

Project 9: Use Computer Models or Simulations

10 Construct and Explain Systems

Systems can be quite complicated. Take our political system, for example. A basic understanding of it is that there are three branches of government, each watching the other to make sure there is no abuse of power. In practice, we know it is far more complex than this. Because many systems are so complex, from ecosystems to the Earth's climate to the solar system, having the ability to analyze complicated systems and describe them concisely and accurately is a valuable skill.

We start small with students, asking them to understand ecosystems, how the economy works, systems of equations, or what system to use in order to write a clear essay. We ask students to explain systems, or write them, or to be able to explain them visually. By being able to understand a system, students are able to see both the big picture as well as the little details. Usually when people fail at systems, it is because they either do not see the big picture or do not understand how the details are put together to create it. Understanding systems is a valuable skill for students to possess indeed.

The Business Plan

In this project, students will work in groups to create a business plan, which they will present to a panel of investors. The business should be a valuable addition to the students' town or city. Students' business plans should be typed and include a thorough description of the business (see Handout 10.2). Students' presentations to the panel should be no longer than 10 minutes, include a visual aid and a logo for their business, and summarize their business plan. Group members should present themselves in a professional manner, speak with confidence, and be prepared to answer follow-up questions from the panel. The panel will select the business idea that it feels was the best presented and makes the most sense for the city.

The panel should be made up of a group of adults, such as members of the local chamber of commerce, local businessmen or politicians (e.g., board members, city council members), parents with a business background, district or school staff, business majors from a local college or university, members of DECA from the local high school, or local bankers.

Materials

- ▸ Project Outline: The Business Plan (student copies)
- ▸ Suggested Timeline
- ▸ Lesson: Why Do We Have Businesses?
- ▸ Handout 10.1: Building Your Business (student copies)
- ▸ Handout 10.2: Creating Your Business Plan (student copies)
- ▸ Product Rubric: The Business Plan (student copies)

PROJECT OUTLINE

The Business Plan

Big Idea

Successful businesses are well planned.

Essential Question

How do you build a successful business?

Deliverables

You will work in a group to create a business plan, which you will present to a panel of investors. The business should be a valuable addition to the your town or city. Your typed business plan should include a thorough description of the business (see Handout 10.2). Your presentation to the panel should:

- ▶ be no longer than 10 minutes,
- ▶ include a visual aid of some sort, and
- ▶ include a logo for the business.

Your presentation must summarize your business plan by including the following information:

- ▶ What is the product or service you offer?
- ▶ Where are you planning to locate the business, and why?
- ▶ Who will be your primary customers?
- ▶ How are you going to market the product?
- ▶ Why do you think this business is going to be successful?

Remember: You are trying to convince the panel that your business will be good for the community. You and your group members should present yourselves in a professional manner, speak with confidence, and be prepared to answer follow-up questions from the panel. The panel will select the business idea that it feels was the best presented and makes the most sense for the city.

Project 10: Construct and Explain Systems

Project Outline: The Business Plan, *continued*

Constraints

Your business plan must identify:

▸ an existing and available location for you to build your business, and

▸ your key customers and how you are going to attract them to your business.

SUGGESTED TIMELINE

DAY				
1 Introduce the project and conduct Lesson: Why Do We Have Businesses? *Ask.*	**2** Divide students into groups and have teams brainstorm possible business ideas (see Handout 10.1). *Imagine.*	**3** Have teams brainstorm possible business ideas (see Handout 10.1). *Imagine.*	**4** Have teams choose their business ideas. *Imagine.*	**5** Have teams begin their business plans (see Handout 10.2). *Plan.*
6 Have teams continue their business plans. *Plan.*	**7** Have teams continue their business plans. *Plan.*	**8** Have teams continue their business plans. *Plan.*	**9** Have teams continue their business plans. *Plan.*	**10** Have teams continue their business plans. *Plan.*
11 Have teams develop their presentations. *Create.*	**12** Have teams develop their presentations. *Create.*	**13** Have teams develop their presentations. *Create.*	**14** Have teams practice their presentations. *Improve.*	**15** Have teams present to the panel.

Why Do We Have Businesses?

1. Ask students to name some of the prominent businesses in your town or city, including grocery stores, restaurants, clothing stores, hardware stores, service centers (e.g., air conditioning and computer repair), auto shops, entertainment, etc.

2. Ask: *Why do you think we have these businesses?* Elicit responses. Guide students to understand that most businesses fill a need in their surrounding community.

3. Ask: *How does location affect a business?* Elicit responses. Guide students to understand that:

   ▶ higher traffic areas might be better for business,

   ▶ the convenience of getting to a business might help (e.g., the business is accessible by major roads, sidewalks, or public transportation),

   ▶ a business's proximity to other stores might help attract customers,

   ▶ some businesses that don't have a lot of foot traffic might not need a prime location, and

   ▶ having more than one location means a business is close to many people.

4. Ask: *Do you know of any business in our town/city that closed? Why do you suppose it went out of business?* Elicit responses. Guide students to understand that businesses can close for many reasons, such as having:

   ▶ too much competition,

   ▶ inferior product(s),

   ▶ a bad location,

   ▶ a product or service that became obsolete,

   ▶ a negative reputation, or

   ▶ poor customer service.

5. Explain that students will have to keep many factors in mind as they plan their businesses if they want to ensure that their businesses are successful.

HANDOUT 10.1

Building Your Business

Directions: In order to build a successful business that benefits your community, you will need to determine what your community's needs are and the best location for your business, among other factors. Some things to consider when building your business include:

1. Is there another local business that provides a similar product/service?

2. Why would people want to buy this product/service?

3. Is there a market for your business?

4. What are similar businesses in the area, and have they been successful?

5. What would be a prime location for this sort of business?

6. Would there be repeat customers?

7. Would you have to have a large work staff, and would they have to be specially trained?

8. How much will it cost to start this business?

9. How will you reach potential customers for this business?

10. Is your business's product/service seasonal?

Name: _____ Date: _____

HANDOUT 10.2

Creating Your Business Plan

Directions: There are five questions every business must answer:
1. What is the business?
2. Who is the business trying to sell to?
3. Where will your business be located?
4. How will you market your product to customers?
5. Why should someone invest in your business?

In order to have a successful business, you must form a business plan that addresses these questions. The answers to these questions will form your business plan. Use a separate sheet of paper as needed. Remember: Your final business plan needs to be typed.

What Is the Business?

1. What are you selling, or what service are you offering?

2. What leads you to believe this service/product is something people in the community would be interested in? (You can perform a survey to gather information if you choose.)

3. Is there any competition from other businesses for what you are offering? How will you compete against them by standing out from the others?

Handout 10.2: Creating Your Business Plan, *continued*

Who Is the Business Trying to Sell to?

1. Who is likely to be your ideal customer?

2. How have you identified that customer?

3. Is there a chance that you can reach other customers who do not fit this profile?

Where Will Your Business Be Located?

1. Do you need to have a physical space for your business (e.g., a store customers can visit), or can it be run out of an office?

2. Where would be the ideal place in town to locate your business?

Project 10: Construct and Explain Systems

Handout 10.2: Creating Your Business Plan, *continued*

3. How will this location increase the chances of getting customers?

How Will You Market Your Product to Customers?

1. How will people learn about your business and what you have to offer?

2. What will the price be for your product, and how does this compare to prices of your competitors?

3. What will you offer in the way of customer service and quality control?

Why Should Someone Invest in Your Business?

1. How much money do you think would be needed to get your business up and running?

Handout 10.2: Creating Your Business Plan, *continued*

2. What are your key strengths that would attract someone to invest in your business?

3. What are the weaknesses of your business as compared to your competitors, and how do you plan on overcoming these?

Project 10: Construct and Explain Systems

PRODUCT RUBRIC

The Business Plan

	Business Plan	Organization	Presentation
Great	Business plan addresses in detail the five questions that the business plan covers. Business plan uses many examples to provide a clear picture of what the business will look like and how it will compete with others. Business plan provides a complete overview of the business, addressing concerns an investor might have.	Business plan looks professional; there are no typos or misspellings. Business plan is easy to follow with a clear table of contents. Business plan is typed in the correct format.	Group presents itself in a professional manner, showing maturity throughout the presentation. Group members consistently speak with confidence. Group is able to answer questions clearly and confidently, providing additional detail for the investors.
Good	Business plan addresses in detail the five questions that the business plan covers, but lacks detail in some areas. Business plan uses examples to provide a picture of what the business will look like and how it will compete with others, but more information could be provided. Business plan provides an overview of the business, addressing most concerns an investor might have.	Business plan looks professional with only a few typos or misspellings. Business plan has a table of contents that directs the reader, but it is not as organized as could be. Most of the business plan is typed in the correct format.	Group presents itself in a professional manner, but not throughout the entire presentation. Group members speak with confidence most of the time, but are not consistent throughout. Group is able to answer most questions with confidence, but does not necessarily provide additional detail for the investors.

Product Rubric: The Business Plan, *continued*

	Business Plan	**Organization**	**Presentation**
Needs improvement	Business plan does not address all five of the questions that the business plan covers. Business plan does not use many examples to provide a picture of what the business will look like and how it will compete with others. Business plan does not provide a complete overview of the business; it does not address concerns an investor might have.	Business plan looks unprofessional; there are many typos and/or misspellings. Business plan is not easy to follow, and/or there is no table of contents. Business plan is not typed in the correct format.	Group does not present itself in a professional manner, showing lack of maturity throughout the presentation. Group members do not speak with confidence. Group is not able to answer questions with confidence, lacking any additional detail for the investors.

Project 10: Construct and Explain Systems

DEVELOP YOUR OWN STEM PROJECTS

You can develop your own projects through the cycle depicted in Figure 7.

Define a Problem

Defining a problem can be handled in many different ways depending on the needs of the class and curriculum. One option is to base it on standards. Consider the Common Core Standards in math and language arts and the Next Generation Science Standards (NGSS). You could choose one of these as the basis of your problem. For example, here is a fifth-grade science standard from the NGSS:

> 5 ESS1-1 Support an argument that the apparent brightness of the sun and stars is due to their relative distances from the Earth.

One could easily construct a project from this problem, having students create a model that shows the relative distances of the sun and nearby stars. Students could even create a demonstration using flashlights that show the varying brightness of these objects as a result of distance.

You could also start with a national STEM learning goal, such as those that make up the structure of this book. Alternatively, you could consider 21st-century skills, such as collaboration and teamwork, creativity and imagination, critical thinking, problem solving, oral and written communication skills, social responsibility and citizenship, technology literacy, and initiative. You could choose from one or more of these areas and

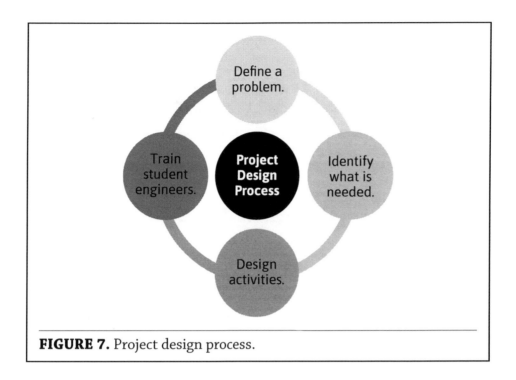

FIGURE 7. Project design process.

develop a project. For example, if you wanted to focus on oral communication, you would have to design your project so that the final product required students to give an oral presentation to an authentic audience.

Yet another way to define a project is by exploring an authentic, real-world problem. Say there is an opioid problem in your school district, or your school is trying to figure out an effective way to run its recycling program. You could take either of these real-world situations and ask students to develop solutions.

Identify What Is Needed

The best way to figure out what is needed for a project is to start at the end. What do you want students to ideally turn in at the end of the project? What would this product look like or involve? Everything stems from this product, including the skills needed to accomplish it and the lessons you will need to teach in order for students to understand what they are doing. You want to have a general idea of what this product is going to look like, but you should not be so detailed that there is little student choice. As much as possible, you should provide students with choices in their products. This is where creativity comes into play as well as student empowerment. Providing students with choice engages them in the learning and will probably lead to a better quality product.

Once you have decided what the product is going to be, you can create the rubric that is going to evaluate it. This is where you set the performance criteria. This should be based on whatever way you chose to define the problem. For instance, if you are focusing on a very specific content standard, this should be reflected in the rubric. However, if you instead decided to focus on a 21st-century skill, the criteria for how to evaluate it need to be laid out in the rubric.

Design Activities

Once the product is put into place, you can backward build the rest of the project. I actually like to use a calendar like you see at the beginning of the projects in this book, putting the final product at the end and then building outward from there. For instance, if the project we were having students work on had a final product of a portfolio, I would have to consider what skills students need to employ and what information they need to find in order to complete the project.

If I were doing a project where students had to create a new mousetrap, one that did not harm the mouse, I would start with the completed mousetrap and then build backward from there. It might look like Figure 8.

This would be plotted out step by step until I reached the beginning of the project when it is being introduced to students. Then, I would go back and determine how much time I would need for each of step and plug the steps into a calendar. The final step is to reverse the order and make sure the project is following the engineering design process (see Figure 9).

Train Student Engineers

Now that you have the project figured out and the product determined, the most challenging part occurs. This is where the teacher has to train his or her student engineers. This means making sure that students have a firm understanding of the how the engineering design process works because it will be the backbone of every STEM project.

Part of this training may include how to work effectively in groups, because STEM projects often require students to have partners or multiple team members. No matter students' age, it would be wrong to assume that

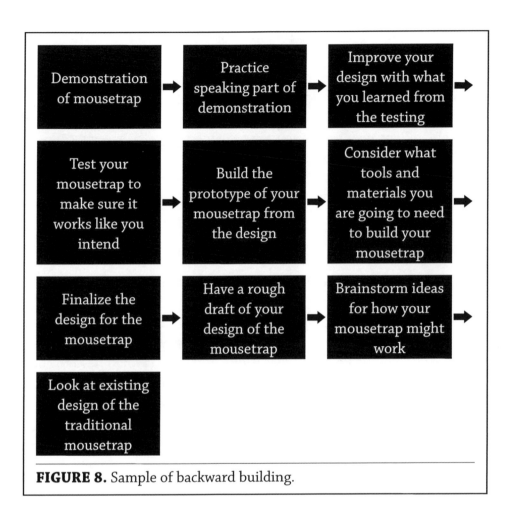

FIGURE 8. Sample of backward building.

they already know how to work with others successfully in the group setting. You will want to make sure to take some time to practice team-working skills and have guidelines for proper group behavior and expectations. You also need to determine ways to evaluate students not just on the overall product produced by the group, but also on what each student's contribution to that product was. If two students turn in the same work, but one contributed 90% of the work, it is not fair to give both an equal grade.

The role of the teacher shifts from being in front of the room, to acting as a coach from the side. It involves conversations with students and keen observation skills to determine when a group or student needs some help, and when you need to let them figure something out for themselves. Part of this is determining how to best use time and space—time in the form of opportunities for students to test and improve their results, and space in the form of learning without interference of the teacher. The best learning

DAY				
1 Introduce the project; review the design of the original mousetrap. *Ask.*	**2** Introduce students to the engineering design process. Allow them to begin brainstorming ideas. *Ask/Imagine.*	**3** Students begin to design their new mousetrap, conducting research to make sure it does not already exist. *Imagine/Plan.*	**4** Students finish designing their new mousetrap. *Plan.*	**5** Students create a list of materials needed to make the model of the mousetrap. *Plan.*
6 Students construct model of mousetrap. *Create.*	**7** Students construct model of mousetrap. *Create.*	**8** Students test mousetrap and make any improvements they think are needed. *Improve.*	**9** Students finish construction of model of mousetrap and test to make sure it works as intended. *Improve.*	**10** Students practice the speaking part of their demonstrations. *Improve.*
11 Students demonstrate their mousetraps.				

FIGURE 9. Sample project calendar. Adapted from *10 Performance-Based Projects for the Science Classroom* (p. 99), by T. Stanley, 2017, Waco, TX: Prufrock Press. Copyright 2017 by Prufrock Press. Adapted with permission.

is discovery learning, which, as a teacher, means sometimes figuring out how to get out of students' way.

Your role is to manage the project, not determine its path. You will need to figure out what skills students might need to have before they can be successful. For instance, if the project calls for students to conduct interviews, do they have the knowledge of how to do these, or are there tips and guidelines you can point them to in order to make their chances for meaningful success that much greater? Keep in mind that most of the heavy lifting should be done by the students.

REFERENCES

Advancement Courses. (2015). *The engineering design process: The 4 key steps to STEM teaching and learning* [Web log post]. Retrieved from https://www.advancementcourses.com/blog/the-engineering-design-process-the-4-key-steps-to-stem-teaching-and-learning

Boaler, J. (2002). Learning from teaching: Exploring the relationship between reform curriculum and equity. *Journal for Research in Mathematics Education, 33,* 239–258.

Buck Institute for Education. (n.d.). *Why PBL?* Retrieved from https://www.bie.org/about/why_pbl

Condliffe, B. (2017). *Project-based learning: A literature review* [Working paper]. New York, NY: MDRC.

Creative Learning Exchange. (2016). *Using system dynamics and systems thinking (SD/ST) tools and learning strategies to build science, technology, engineering, and math excellence.* Retrieved from http://www.clexchange.org/curriculum/standards/stem.asp

Deitering, S. (2016). *Is project based learning a more effective way of teaching than traditional teaching?* (Master's thesis, Northwestern College, Orange City, IA). Retrieved from https://nwcommons.nwciowa.edu/education_masters/12

Dintersmith, T., & Whiteley, G. (2015). *Most likely to succeed* [Motion picture]. United States: One Potato Productions.

Engineering is Elementary. (2018). *The engineering design process.* Retrieved from https://www.eie.org/overview/engineering-design-process

Graduate Management Admission Council. (2018). *Employers seek communication skills in new hires*. Retrieved from https://www.mba.com/mbas-and-business-masters/articles/your-career-path/employers-seek-communications-skills

International Technology and Engineering Educators Association. (2016). *About*. Retrieved from https://www.iteea.org/About.aspx

Mathison, S., & Feeman, M. (1997). *The logic of interdisciplinary studies*. Presented at the Annual Meeting of the American Educational Research Association, Chicago, IL.

Menzies, V., Hewitt, C., Kokotsaki, D., Collyer, C., & Wiggins, A. (2016). *Project-based learning: Evaluation report and executive summary*. London, England: Education Endowment Foundation.

Partnership for 21st Century Skills. (2016). *P21 framework definitions*. Washington, DC: Author.

Scholastic. (n.d.). *Building abstract thinking through math*. Retrieved from https://www.scholastic.com/teachers/articles/teaching-content/building-abstract-thinking-through-math

Stanley, T. (2015). *Creating life-long learners: Using project-based management to teach 21st century skills*. Thousand Oaks, CA: Corwin.

Stanley, T. (2017). *10 performance-based projects for the science classroom*. Waco, TX: Prufrock Press.

Stanley, T. (2018). *When smart kids underachieve in school: Practical solutions for teachers*. Waco, TX: Prufrock Press.

Thomas, J. W. (2000). *A review of research on project-based learning*. San Rafael, CA: Autodesk Foundation.

ABOUT THE AUTHOR

Todd Stanley is author of many teacher education books, including *Project-Based Learning for Gifted Students: A Handbook for the 21st-Century Classroom* and *Performance-Based Assessment for 21st-Century Skills*. He was a classroom teacher for 18 years, teaching students as young as second graders and as old as high school seniors, and was a National Board Certified teacher. He helped create a gifted academy for grades 5–8, which employs inquiry-based learning, project-based learning, and performance-based assessment. He is currently the gifted services coordinator for Pickerington Local School District in Ohio, where he lives with his wife, Nicki, and two daughters, Anna and Abby. You can follow him on Twitter @the_gifted_guy or visit his website at https://www.thegiftedguy.com.

NEXT GENERATION SCIENCE STANDARDS ALIGNMENT

Project	Next Generation Science Standards
Project 2	*Note.* Standards for this project will vary based upon students' selected topics.
Project 3	*Note.* Standards for this project will vary based upon students' selected topics.
Project 4	*Note.* Standards for this project will vary based upon students' selected topics.

Project	Subject	Standards
Project 2, *continued*	ELA, *continued*	SL.7.5 Include multimedia components and visual displays in presentations to clarify claims and findings and emphasize salient points.
		W.8.1 Write arguments to support claims with clear reasons and relevant evidence.
		SL.8.4 Present claims and findings, emphasizing salient points in a focused, coherent manner with relevant evidence, sound valid reasoning, and well-chosen details; use appropriate eye contact, adequate volume, and clear pronunciation.
		SL.8.5 Integrate multimedia and visual displays into presentations to clarify information, strengthen claims and evidence, and add interest.
	Math	*Note.* Standards for this project will vary based upon students' selected topics.
Project 3	ELA	SL.6.4 Present claims and findings, sequencing ideas logically and using pertinent descriptions, facts, and details to accentuate main ideas or themes; use appropriate eye contact, adequate volume, and clear pronunciation.
		SL.6.5 Include multimedia components (e.g., graphics, images, music, sound) and visual displays in presentations to clarify information.
		SL.7.4 Present claims and findings, emphasizing salient points in a focused, coherent manner with pertinent descriptions, facts, details, and examples; use appropriate eye contact, adequate volume, and clear pronunciation.
		SL.7.5 Include multimedia components and visual displays in presentations to clarify claims and findings and emphasize salient points.

161

Project	Subject	Standards
Project 3, *continued*	ELA, *continued*	SL.8.4 Present claims and findings, emphasizing salient points in a focused, coherent manner with relevant evidence, sound valid reasoning, and well-chosen details; use appropriate eye contact, adequate volume, and clear pronunciation.
		SL.8.5 Integrate multimedia and visual displays into presentations to clarify information, strengthen claims and evidence, and add interest.
	Math	*Note.* Standards for this project will vary based upon students' selected topics.
Project 4	ELA	*Note.* Standards for this project will vary based upon students' selected topics.
Project 5	Math	7.EE.B Solve real-life and mathematical problems using numerical and algebraic expressions and equations.
Project 6	Math	*Note.* Standards for this project will vary based upon students' selected topics.
Project 7	ELA	W.6.1 Write arguments to support claims with clear reasons and relevant evidence.
		SL.6.4 Present claims and findings, sequencing ideas logically and using pertinent descriptions, facts, and details to accentuate main ideas or themes; use appropriate eye contact, adequate volume, and clear pronunciation.
		SL.6.5 Include multimedia components (e.g., graphics, images, music, sound) and visual displays in presentations to clarify information.
		W.7.1 Write arguments to support claims with clear reasons and relevant evidence.
		SL.7.4 Present claims and findings, emphasizing salient points in a focused, coherent manner with pertinent descriptions, facts, details, and examples; use appropriate eye contact, adequate volume, and clear pronunciation.

Project	Subject	Standards
Project 7, *continued*	ELA, *continued*	SL.7.5 Include multimedia components and visual displays in presentations to clarify claims and findings and emphasize salient points.
		W.8.1 Write arguments to support claims with clear reasons and relevant evidence.
		SL.8.4 Present claims and findings, emphasizing salient points in a focused, coherent manner with relevant evidence, sound valid reasoning, and well-chosen details; use appropriate eye contact, adequate volume, and clear pronunciation.
		SL.8.5 Integrate multimedia and visual displays into presentations to clarify information, strengthen claims and evidence, and add interest.
	Math	*Note.* Standards for this project will vary based upon students' selected topics.
Project 8	ELA	W.6.1 Write arguments to support claims with clear reasons and relevant evidence.
		W.6.7 Conduct short research projects to answer a question, drawing on several sources and refocusing the inquiry when appropriate.
		W.7.1 Write arguments to support claims with clear reasons and relevant evidence.
		W.7.7 Conduct short research projects to answer a question, drawing on several sources and generating additional related, focused questions for further research and investigation.
		W.8.1 Write arguments to support claims with clear reasons and relevant evidence.
		W.8.7 Conduct short research projects to answer a question (including a self-generated question), drawing on several sources and generating additional related, focused questions that allow for multiple avenues of exploration.
Project 9	ELA	W.6.1 Write arguments to support claims with clear reasons and relevant evidence.

Project	Subject	Standards
Project 9, *continued*	ELA, *continued*	SL.6.4 Present claims and findings, sequencing ideas logically and using pertinent descriptions, facts, and details to accentuate main ideas or themes; use appropriate eye contact, adequate volume, and clear pronunciation.
		SL.6.5 Include multimedia components (e.g., graphics, images, music, sound) and visual displays in presentations to clarify information.
		W.7.1 Write arguments to support claims with clear reasons and relevant evidence.
		SL.7.4 Present claims and findings, emphasizing salient points in a focused, coherent manner with pertinent descriptions, facts, details, and examples; use appropriate eye contact, adequate volume, and clear pronunciation.
		SL.7.5 Include multimedia components and visual displays in presentations to clarify claims and findings and emphasize salient points.
		W.8.1 Write arguments to support claims with clear reasons and relevant evidence.
		SL.8.4 Present claims and findings, emphasizing salient points in a focused, coherent manner with relevant evidence, sound valid reasoning, and well-chosen details; use appropriate eye contact, adequate volume, and clear pronunciation.
		SL.8.5 Integrate multimedia and visual displays into presentations to clarify information, strengthen claims and evidence, and add interest.
	Math	*Note.* Standards for this project will vary based upon students' selected topics.
Project 10	ELA	W.6.1 Write arguments to support claims with clear reasons and relevant evidence.

Project	Subject	Standards
Project 10, *continued*	ELA, *continued*	SL.6.4 Present claims and findings, sequencing ideas logically and using pertinent descriptions, facts, and details to accentuate main ideas or themes; use appropriate eye contact, adequate volume, and clear pronunciation.
		SL.6.5 Include multimedia components (e.g., graphics, images, music, sound) and visual displays in presentations to clarify information.
		W.7.1 Write arguments to support claims with clear reasons and relevant evidence.
		SL.7.4 Present claims and findings, emphasizing salient points in a focused, coherent manner with pertinent descriptions, facts, details, and examples; use appropriate eye contact, adequate volume, and clear pronunciation.
		SL.7.5 Include multimedia components and visual displays in presentations to clarify claims and findings and emphasize salient points.
		W.8.1 Write arguments to support claims with clear reasons and relevant evidence.
		SL.8.4 Present claims and findings, emphasizing salient points in a focused, coherent manner with relevant evidence, sound valid reasoning, and well-chosen details; use appropriate eye contact, adequate volume, and clear pronunciation.
		SL.8.5 Integrate multimedia and visual displays into presentations to clarify information, strengthen claims and evidence, and add interest.
	Math	*Note.* Standards for this project will vary based upon students' selected topics.